CITYSPOTS
MARRA

Ethel Davies

Written and photographed by Ethel Davies
Front cover photograph copyright Getty Images

Produced by 183 Books
Design/layout/maps: Chris Lane and Lee Biggadike
Editorial/project management: Stephen York

Published by Thomas Cook Publishing
A division of Thomas Cook Tour Operations Limited
PO Box 227, Units 15/16, Coningsby Road
Peterborough PE3 8SB, United Kingdom
email: books@thomascook.com
www.thomascookpublishing.com
+44 (0) 1733 416477

First edition © 2006 Thomas Cook Publishing
Text © 2006 Thomas Cook Publishing
Maps © 2006 Thomas Cook Publishing
ISBN-13: 978-1-84157-582-7
ISBN-10: 1-84157-582-8
Project Editor: Kelly Anne Pipes
Production/DTP: Steven Collins

Printed and bound in Spain by GraphyCems

CONTENTS

SYMBOLS & ABBREVIATIONS

The following symbols are used throughout this book:

ⓣ telephone   ⓕ fax   ⓦ website address
ⓐ address   ⓛ opening times

The following symbols are used on the maps:
🅗 Tourist Information Office
✈ Airport

Hotels and restaurants are graded by approximate price as follows:
D budget price   **DD** mid-range price   **DDD** expensive
The local currency is the dirham (see page 144)

24-HOUR CLOCK

All times in this book are given in the 24-hour clock system used widely in Europe and in most international transport timetables.

⊙ *The ancient pink-hued buildings of the Medina form the centre of the city*

Introduction

The first thing that a visitor to Marrakech notices is the colour of the city. Everywhere seems to be a salmon-shade of dark pink, whether on the houses of the recent developments near the airport, 21st-century office blocks or the buildings of the old city. Marrakech, the capital of south Morocco in spirit, if no longer in name, is painted the colours of the sub-Saharan desert sands. It is said that each new construction is allowed a choice of only two colours: the pinker hue of the city's famous and historical hotel, the Mamounia, or the slightly more ochre version of the Koutobuia, the tall, graceful minaret that is Marrakech's landmark.

The next thing that becomes apparent to travellers to Marrakech is the wall surrounding the old settlement, or Medina. High and intact, with massive gates set in at intervals along it, this impressive edifice separates the modern European metropolis from the ancient Arab one. UNESCO declared this ancient enclave a World Heritage Site in 1985, in order to guarantee its preservation.

The new city (Guéliz) has broad tree-lined boulevards, a legacy left by the French who occupied Morocco for 44 years, while the old centre is surrounded, seemingly keeping its secrets inside. It's the sense of these mysteries that makes Marrakech so appealing, and once within the Medina, the labyrinth of streets and passageways confuses still further. The ancient centre is relatively small, however, and the local inhabitants are friendly, so it doesn't matter if you get lost – sooner or later you'll find your way.

Just inside the walls is the Jemaa el Fna. A UNESCO 'Heritage of Humanity' site, this huge square is filled with Moroccan characters, selling their wares or demonstrating their skills. At night, the place is packed with locals, clamouring to hear tales from the storytellers as well as watch the various ethnic performers. Dozens of food stalls with benches for diners are packed in against one another, each with its hawker soliciting passers-by for custom. Further in, it's impossible not to get caught up in the various markets, or souks. Shopping is an experience dazzling to the eye, as well as to the pocket. As a general rule, however, don't pay the first asking price. Bargaining is a form of social relationship as well as an economic tool.

Not all of the city's 1.6 million population lives inside the densely packed centre. The Ville Nouveau, the new city, is growing almost daily, with plans to increase the urban development further. Beyond the official city limits is the Palmeraie, once a palm grove and now the most fashionable resort in the area. With exclusive hotels, luxury houses, a golf course and horse riding, this suburb is where both the domestic and foreign wealthy are choosing to build their second homes.

On clear days, especially during the winter, the natural barrier against which the entire region nestles becomes visible. The High Atlas, North Africa's highest mountains, lie just to the south of Marrakech. Mt Toubkal, at 4165 m (13,665 ft), is the tallest peak in the north of the continent and it's possible to ascend to the summit in a couple of days. There are also other destinations in the area that make this region an easy single- or multi-day excursion away from the city.

If being inland in a country with such a long ocean coast is a problem, the seaside resort of Essaouria makes a welcome change from the dry sands of Marrakech. A 2.5-hour bus or taxi ride away, this easy-going blue and white city is known for its battlements, fresh fish and artistic atmosphere.

When to go

Spring and autumn are the most pleasant seasons to visit
Marrakech, as the weather is at its gentlest during these times of
year. To attend the city's most important folk event, the Festival of
Popular Arts, however, you have to brave the heat of June. Even the
relative coolness of winter is pleasant compared to Northern Europe,
although it can rain quite a bit. In the colder months the air is clear,
and snow on the Atlas presents a spectacular backdrop to the city,
which can be skied upon at the mountain resort of Oukaimeden.

SEASONS & CLIMATE
Located in the plains below North Africa's highest range, springtime
is pleasant, with temperatures on average in the mid-20s °C (70s °F).

There can be a great deal of precipitation during the earlier part of the season, although plants and flowers flourish in the rain. Summers are hot and dry, with the thermometer reaching about 38°C (100°F) during the day, and rarely going below 20°C (68°F) at night. Rising haze obscures visibility and can last into the autumn, although the temperature drops back down into the 20s °C (70s °F) as the year progresses.

In the winter, clear days offer spectacular glimpses of the snow-covered Atlas Mountains. Although not warm by Moroccan standards, at an average of 17°C (62°F), and with darker and wetter days than the rest of the year, winter in Marrakech can still be a pleasant break for Northern European or American visitors.

◉ *Renowned Moroccan horsemanship is put on display during July's Fantasia*

ANNUAL EVENTS

Morocco has several celebrations throughout the country, including those intended only for Muslim worshippers. Here are some of the more popular events in Marrakech that have an international appeal. For more information see Ⓦ www.morocco.com/culture/celebrations

January
Marrakech Marathon With Morocco producing champion long-distance runners, the Marrakech marathon attracts thousands of participants. Ⓦ www.marathon-marrakech.com

June
Gnaoua Festival The four-day music festival held annually in Essaouira (170 km/105 miles west of Marrakech; see page 126 and page 134) is dedicated to this traditional melodic form, as well as fusion with western styles of music and internationally known performers. Ⓦ www.festival-gnaoua.co.ma

July
Marrakech Popular Arts Festival The city's most important folklore event celebrates traditional Moroccan cultural forms and includes singing and dancing. Events take place across the Medina, but are centred on the Badi Palace, which is packed with performers, dancers and those being entertained for the duration of the folk festival. Most spectacular of all is the display of horsemanship at the Fantasia, held every night of the festival just outside the city walls near Bab Jdid.

August
Setti Fatma Moussem Although this moussem, or pilgrimage to a holy

PUBLIC HOLIDAYS

Muslim holidays (*) can vary by as much as a month, as they are based on the lunar calendar

New Year's Day 1 Jan
Tabaski (Feast of Sacrifice) (2 days) 10 Jan 2006*
Independence Manifesto Day 11 Jan
Islamic New Year 31 Jan 2006*
The Prophet's Birthday (2 days) 10 April 2006*
Labour Day 1 May
HM the Queen's Birthday 27 May
Throne Day 30 July
Assumption Day 14 Aug
Revolution Day 20 Aug
The King's Birthday 21 Aug
Ramadan 23 Sept–22 Oct 2006*
Independence Day 18 Nov
Eid El Fitr (2 days) 23 Oct 2006*

shrine, is dedicated to the saint Setti Fatma, this event in the High Atlas village (see page 119–120) is more of a fair than a religious event.

September/October/November
Ramadan For a period of one month, devout Muslims adhere to the restrictions of Ramadan – no eating, smoking, drinking or sexual activity from dawn till dusk. It's best not to plan any lunch dates during this time. For more information see Ⓦ en.wikipedia.org
The Marrakech International Film Festival (see page 12).

Marrakech International Film Festival

Four years after being established, the annual Marrakech International Film Festival is on cinema's 'A' list. Attracting famous actors from all over the world, the event claims it is a meeting point of East and West. In practice, it is more of a North African Cannes, with glamour, parties and even royal patronage, as shown by King Mohamed VI's sponsorship and keen interest.

Since its opening in the autumn of 2001, the festival has gone from strength to strength. Juries have been presided over by well-known western personalities such as the French director Jean-Jacques Annaud, the French actor Jeanne Moreau and the English director Alan Parker. Additionally, honours were given to the Scottish actor Sean Connery, Italian actor Claudia Cardinale and the American director Martin Scorsese. African filmmakers are also represented, both in their presence and their work, and the cinema of the Far East is also shown. More and more mainstream cinema interests are getting involved. The festival is now held in November, drifting away from its original September date to avoid Ramadan.

Marrakech itself is the venue. When audiences are too large for the smaller cinemas, outdoor screens are set up in the grounds of the enormous ruins of the Badi Palace, as well as the huge square of the Jemaa el Fna. As the festival gains in popularity, and its audience continues to increase beyond the already attending numbers of over 100,000, more of the city will be used as impromptu exhibition areas.

Cinema has long been important to Morocco. Hollywood discovered that the scenery of the country could double for other less accessible locations, and began to come to the country to start making movies. In 1952 Orson Welles arrived in Marrakech's seaside neighbour of Essaouira, where he made his film *Othello*. This event, and the director, are commemorated in the naming of one of the city's squares as place Orson Welles. A few years later, Alfred Hitchcock decided to use the Hotel Mamounia in his movie *The Man Who Knew Too Much*. The turning point in Morocco's career as a film set came in 1962, when David Lean chose its desert as the location for *Lawrence of Arabia*.

Since then movies have been made here on a regular basis. Morocco stands in for any number of places, such as Israel in *Jesus of Nazareth*, an unnamed Middle Eastern country in *Jewel of the Nile*, somewhere in Asia Minor in *Alexander* and even Tibet, in Martin Scorsese's film of the life of the Dalai Lama, *Kundun*. Further south and closer to the real desert is the town of Ouarzazate. Here, a film studio grows ever larger, hosting bigger and bigger productions. Between the cheap labour available, from both technicians and extras, the political stability and the government's (and King's) sympathy to the industry, making movies here is a real alternative to production in more expensive places. It's not surprising that more and more of the films shown in the Marrakech International Film Festival, whether of African origin or not, were actually filmed in Morocco.

Marrakech International Film Festival ⓐ Festival International du Film de Marrakech, c/o Société GCC, 19 rue Lauriston, 75116 Paris, France ⓣ 33 1 5364 0525 ⓕ 33 1 5364 0524.

The festival's website was being updated at the time of writing, but in the meantime information is available at ⓦ www.maghrebarts.ma/cinema/fifm/main.html

History

Marrakech has always been a city of Berbers, an ancient assembly of members of unknown Euro-Asiatic origin, residing primarily in the Atlas Mountains. The history of the area comprises a continual wave of invasions from both internal and external powers. Yet the heritage remains to this day, with about 75 per cent of the population descended from Berber tribes.

When the seagoing Phoenicians first arrived on the Atlantic coast in the 12th century BC, the Berbers were already well

established, and they remained the main racial group throughout subsequent foreign incursions. By this point, the region had become a spot of rich pickings, as it held an important position on the trade routes between central Africa and the sea coast. The early history of Morocco is a series of raids by visiting conquerors such as the Romans, Byzantines and Arabs.

In the 11th century, a group of Berber tribes banded together to form the Almoravids. Strong, resilient and used to the harsh

The magnificence of the Saadian rule is apparent in the tombs of their princes

conditions of mountain life, the group set up camp at the base of one of the major crossroads of the Atlas Mountains. This settlement became a fixed point on the trade route, and became known as 'Marra Kouch'. Historians do not agree on the meaning, but one possible explanation is 'the Land of the Kouchmen' (a tribe of black warriors coming from Mauretania, the country that once included Morocco as one of its territories). Adhering to the Muslim faith that most Berbers had adopted during the Arab conquests, the Almoravids began to cede adjoining lands and soon had an Islamic empire that reached as far as Lisbon to the north, West Africa to the west, Algeria to the east, and all of Morocco to the south. The capital Marrakech flourished and became a magnificent city, although all that remains of this glory today is the Qoubba El Badiyin fountain.

The city's history began to follow a pattern, with one tribe conquering, flourishing, developing the city, going into decline and then falling to the next invaders. The Almohads in the mid-12th century were next, defeating the Almoravids, destroying the old Marrakech but rebuilding a beautiful one in its place. Many of the city's current structures, including its icon, the graceful minaret of the Koutoubia, were built at this time. By 1276, however, the last of the Almohads were overcome by the next ruling tribe, the Merenids.

Marrakech was out of favour with the Merenids, however, and the new imperial cities of the north, including Fes, took precedence. This decline continued until the Merenids, weakened by internal issues and continual Christian attacks from the Iberian peninsula, were overwhelmed by the next tribe, the Saadians, in the mid-16th century.

The ruling sultans returned to Marrakech, moving the court and reinvesting in the city, and it began to blossom once more. Arts and architecture flourished, and many details still visible today sprang from this era. However, after the death of the Saadian sultan in 1607, chaos returned. For more than 60 years civil war raged, until an Arab prince arrived to settle the conflict. Though his reign was not marked by anything particularly notable, he created the bloodline that remains, his descendants ruling Morocco today.

Marrakech remained medieval until 1856, when the sultan Abdel Rahman, anxious to modernise his nation and afraid of France's intentions, signed a free trade agreement with Britain. His signature effectively opened up Morocco to Europe, bringing it into the 19th century, but also priming it once again for conquest. For the next 60 years, France continued to encroach upon the country till finally, in the Treaty of Fes in 1912, the sultan bowed to pressure and allowed Morocco to become a colony of the French.

Subjugation was always going to be tricky, and despite seemingly enlightened policies, like representatives chosen from local people, and significant modernisation of the Marrakech landscape, being under foreign rule was hard for the Moroccans. When the numbers of resident Europeans became enormous, and the gap between lifestyles too much to take, the seeds of an independence movement were sown. In 1953, the anxious French sent Mohammed V into exile, an event that further riled the nation. A period of violence ensued and the King was allowed to return in 1955. By then, however, governing the colony was just too difficult, and France granted Morocco independence in March 1956.

As a constitutional monarchy, with Mohammed V's son, King Hassan II, the first modern ruler of the independent country of Morocco, the country began to stabilise. Today, Hassan's II son, King Mohammed VI, is on the throne, and his priority is to continue the country's development up to 21st-century standard while alleviating its serious poverty issues.

Lifestyle

Marrakech seems exotic and foreign. The mystery and secrecy of life behind its walls applies to its culture as well as to its buildings. Women walk in the streets in all variations of Muslim garb, whether wrapped up completely so that only the eyes are seen, or showing off traces of stomach when wearing of low-slung jeans. Morocco is a Muslim country, effectively and legally. With the exception of a small number of Jews, everyone born here is Muslim and must adhere to its tenets. In theory, for example, flaunting of the restrictions of Ramadan (see events, page 11) can mean imprisonment. (If caught, however, freedom can be bought but the violation is often overlooked.) Islam is avidly practised, but the variety is not fundamentalist. The call to prayer is broadcast from various minarets throughout the city five times a day, the first at a very early 05.15.

● *Adhering to Muslim traditions doesn't mean the city lacks colour*

Often the slightly different timings create a strange, not quite echoing song, with the varying pitches and voices overlapping. Nondescript doors that are closed most of the time are opened during prayer times, and for non-believers, it's possible to catch a glimpse of reverent men bowing on their prayer mats just beyond. Mosques are not open to non-Muslims.

Yet for all this fervour, foreigners are accepted and welcomed. Allowances are granted to tourists that might not be offered locals. The wearing of shorts and going around with bare shoulders is just about tolerated for visitors, but rarely seen among Marrakchis. Discretion is advised as to attire and respect is certainly something that the Moroccans appreciate. Perhaps it's best to leave more casual clothing to the resorts outside the city.

For all its aspirations and plans, Morocco is still pretty much a developing country. Advice given when visiting developing countries apply to Marrakech, such as drinking bottled water rather than tap, or being cautious eating street food (the stalls at the Jemaa el Fna are an exception, as they are generally licensed). More streets in the Medina are becoming paved, but quite a few are still dirt and turn into muddy quagmires when it rains. Many people are poor, especially in the countryside, and illiteracy is still a serious issue. Even those children lucky enough to go to school, and the number is up to almost 50 per cent for girls, usually finish their education by the age of 13.

What seems expensive to a local appears cheap to western tourists. Prices are low here and goods and services cost relatively little. Many visitors come for extended periods, finding their money lasting longer than they expected. Alternatively, it's also possible to buy a lot more in the souks. Eventually, though, the weight or bulk restrictions of carrying all one's purchases might limit buying power more than the price!

Culture

From the mass of people gathering to watch performances in the old city's main square to the exquisite artistic detailing suddenly appearing out of nowhere on the walls, Marrakech is a city of the arts. The Medina's huge open area, the Jemaa El Fna, is the location of daily, and nightly, expressions of Morocco's living culture. Here, performances, varying from snake charmers to traditional transvestite dancers, occur every day and night. Upholding old traditions while continuing to enthral each new generation, this event is one of Marrakech's most important cultural legacies. The fundamentalist Islamic belief that art should be representational rather than realistic has led to an explosion of beautiful abstract creations, and these can be found in many locations throughout the city. Old royal residences like the Bahia Palace are covered with such forms and have now been turned into museums. The Saadian tombs are surprisingly cheerful, with magnificent mosaics and superb wood carvings surrounding the outdoor graveyard. Some private buildings have been converted to areas open to the public, such as Bert Flint's home, now the Tiskiwin Museum, and the Ben Youssef Medersa Koranic school. Other exhibitions worth a visit include the Dar Si Said Museum, the Museum of Marrakech and the Museum of Islamic Art hiding within the exquisite Majorelle Gardens.

The recent completion of the Opera in Guéliz (the new city) offers Marrakech's performing arts a new home, although an actual opera company has yet to be established. Often known as the Theatre Royal, the Philharmonic Orchestra of Morocco uses this hall as its Marrakech venue. Cinema is very popular, with two movie theatres

▶ *The Bahia Palace is filled with typical representational art forms*

within the Medina and three in Guéliz, catering to the populace's wish to see films from both Hollywood and the rest of the world. The Marrakech International Film Festival (see page 12) acknowledges the country's adoration of the medium. Other celebrations occur regularly, including the Festival of Popular Arts in June. This festivity is well known for its display of horsemanship, the Fantasia. Outside of these dates, a touristy but still impressive recreation of these equestrian skills can be seen at Chez Ali, just outside Marrakech.

Art can be found in several areas of the souks (markets), with many craftsmen producing work that rises above the general tourist kitsch. More formally, however, some Moroccan artists are represented in art galleries across the city. Places such as La Qoubba Galerie d'Art in the Medina and Galerie Bleu, in Guéliz, present contemporary works in appropriate surroundings. More casual and less pretentious is the Ensemble Artisanal, not far from the town hall, a series of workshops used by traditional craftsmen.

Although Moroccan music is internationally acknowledged, much of it in association with western rock (Jimmy Page and Robert Plant have recorded with Gnaoua musicians), there are almost no regular venues in Marrakech to hear it performed. The Jemaa has its share of musicians, although many of them stop and start according to the number of coins thrown at them.

ADMISSION CHARGES

Charges are levied at all Marrakech's galleries, museums and palaces, but admission fees are very low.

▶ *Souks are an experience, even if you aren't tempted to buy*

MAKING THE MOST OF
MAKING THE MOST OF
Marrakech

Shopping

One of the very best things to do in Marrakech is to go shopping. Whether just looking or actually purchasing, browsing and comparing items are great pleasures. These activities can easily take days and it's possible to visit the city and do nothing else.

Souks are defined as 'marketplaces in northern Africa or the

BARGAINING

In many of Marrakech's shops and virtually all of the souks, negotiating the cost of an item is mandatory. Vendors will almost never give the real asking price of goods at the beginning of the discussion. It's up to the purchaser to counter-offer, and here begins not only the fun, but also an important aspect of social interaction. In some cases, depending on how fierce the negotiations get, the final price can be as little as one tenth of the opening bid. A general rule of thumb in knowing how far to go is when the seller simply refuses to lower the amount any further. At this point, the buyer can decide if the price is acceptable or, if still too high, walk away. On returning, if the price still hasn't changed, then it's clear the final figure has been put on the table. An extra caveat however, is that sometimes bargaining can be a matter of saving face, so it might be worthwhile to include an extra element in the proceedings, such as offering to buy two items instead of one, or settling for a less expensive object.

▶ *The sellers themselves bring character to the myriad city stalls*

Middle East', and the ones in this city are some of the best in the Arab world. In the centre of the Medina are tiny maze-like streets made even narrower by the masses of goods on display. Seemingly chaotic, the different souks are divided and classified, more or less, by the goods they sell. The main market place is just north of the Jemaa el Fna, and some of the specialities include dried fruit and nuts (Souk Kchacha), carpets (Souk Joutia Zrabi), leather goods (Souk Cherratine) and dyed yarns (Souk Sebbaghine). Venturing further into the labyrinth, past the stalls, it's possible to wander into the areas where the craftsmen are working, producing the goods seen

● *With stalls specialising in one item, you are always spoilt for choice*

on display. Most of the markets are not fixed price and bargaining is an essential part of the purchasing process. As a guideline, it's worth visiting some of the fixed-price crafts shops, such as the Ensemble Artisanal in the Medina, to find out how much they charge for similar goods. Alternatively, if bargaining is not an option, it might be better to visit some of the more conventional, if ultimately more expensive, stores.

Marrakech has its share of elegant shopping, where price tags are immovable and usually higher than in the markets. Hidden within the souks are shops that offer finer and more exclusive goods than are seen on the outside stalls. Dior has its Marrakech venue within the Mamounia Hotel, while Guéliz houses some exclusive stores that offer antiques, fine fashion and even gourmet pastries.

USEFUL SHOPPING PHRASES

What time do the shops open/close?
A quelle heure ouvrent/ferment les magasins?
Ah kehlur oovr/fehrm leh mahgazhang?

How much is this?
C'est combien?
Cey combyahng?

Can I try this on?
Puis-je essayer ceci?
Pweezh ehssayeh cerssee?

My size is ...
Ma taille (clothes)/
ma pointure (shoes) est ...
Mah tie/mah pooahngtewr ay ...

I'll take this one, thank you
Je prends celui-ci/celle-ci merci
*Zher prahng serlweesi/
sehlsee mehrsee*

Eating & drinking

Although Marrakech has a large number of restaurants, and even more cafés, there is not much of a variety in gastronomic styles. Food on offer tends to consist of Moroccan specialities with a fair number of Italian dishes as an alternative. A few of the more exclusive restaurants bend this rule and offer fine French cuisine; there's even a recently opened Thai eatery. As Morocco is a Muslim country where alcohol consumption is still frowned upon, the places where drinks are served are few and far between. For picnickers, there are several small shops in town that sell drinking water, basic food items and snacks. There is one somewhat larger supermarket at the edge of the Medina at Bab Doukkala, while the big hypermarkets that have a better selection and lower prices are outside central Marrakech, on the roads to Fes and Casablanca.

EATING

Cafés are open from 06.00 (for breakfast) to 23.00 or later. Coffee, pastries and light snacks are available during operating hours. Local eating houses serving the ubiquitous Moroccan dishes are open

PRICE RATING

The restaurant price guides used in the book indicate the approximate cost of a three-course meal for one person, excluding drinks, at the time of writing.

D = up to D160   **DD** = D160–D480   **DDD**= over D480

● *Escape the midday heat in on of Jemaa el Fna's many cafés*

most of the day, and often into the evening. Many of the better restaurants are open evenings only from around 19.00, although some will be open for lunch then close again until dinner.

Eating at the stalls on the Jemaa el Fna Square starts from around 18.00 and goes on to 21.00 or later, and is certainly worth doing at least once. All the food is cooked to order, based on whatever is on display. Some of the impromptu eateries have a huge selection, while others feature fish, soup, goat's meat or any number of specialities.

Although specifically vegetarian food is not part of the Moroccan gastronomic tradition, it's possible to order dishes modified to be meatless. Salads are a regular item on the lunch menu, and some traditional dishes can be prepared with vegetables only. At the stalls on the square, individual ingredients can be requested.

There are no dress codes at any of the casual restaurants. The seating arrangements are pretty much do-it-yourself. At the evening Jemaa eating spots, sit down wherever there is space. The more elegant places, especially at fine hotels such as the Mamounia, require formal attire, sometimes with suit and tie mandatory for men. At these places, the maitre d' will seat customers.

Tipping is common at the more relaxed restaurants, the amount ranging from rounding up the bill to 10 per cent. At the better venues, gratuities will usually be included in the total.

DRINKING

Alcohol consumption is not part of the Muslim tradition. There are a few places in the Medina where it's possible to get a drink at a

⊙ *Tagine is both the name of the conical cooking vessel and of the dish itself* bar, but it's easier to get hold of wine in connection with a meal at some of the more expensive restaurants. In general, liquor is more readily available in the French-influenced Guéliz, or the westernised Palmeraie, than in the Medina.

Marrakech has some of the best orange juice in the world. Oranges grow on the trees surrounding the city. The Jemaa el Fna is full of dozens of vendors selling freshly pressed juice, each shouting for custom.

Coffee is an everyday drink, in plentiful supply in both the Medina and Guéliz. People-watching goes hand in hand with

caffeine consumption and the pavement cafés are full of spectators. Locals come here to read the newspapers and chat with friends.

The Marrakech drink of choice is mint tea. Brewed from daily deliveries of bunches of fresh mint and laden with almost more sugar than water, the beverage is a Moroccan institution. It is served at most hours, refreshing energy levels at midday and finishing a meal off nicely. It also serves as an aid to commerce, brought out in the middle of a bargaining situation, or offered at its successful conclusion.

DO-IT-YOURSELF

Marrakech is not an ideal place for picnicking, as food stores are not plentiful. The city is a bit dusty and the midday heat can get fierce. However, if eating on the green is a necessity, there are parks and gardens just beyond the city walls that have pleasant places to sit.

The stalls at the souks are excellent for dried fruit, nuts, olives and pastries, although more basic foodstuffs are available at the small local mini-marts situated throughout the city. Both of the city's supermarkets are located on the outskirts, Marjane on the Route de Casablanca and du Metro on the route de Fez.

LOCAL SPECIALITIES

Moroccan cuisine is distinctive and delicious, if not terribly varied. Tagine is the best-known dish, a stew of meat or chicken slow cooked and tarted up with apricots, prunes, raisins, citrus fruit or almonds. The platter with a cone-shaped lid bears the same name. It's possible to see rows of these earthenware pots cooking away in many of the restaurants and stalls throughout Marrakech, each with a different variety of tagine. The concoction is usually served up with couscous, a type of semolina ground into small kernels.

This name also applies to another speciality where the grain is smothered in a vegetable or meat sauce. This dish can be bland, so *harissa*, a spicy red tomato-and-varying-degrees-of-chili sauce, is sometimes offered alongside to liven up the mix.

USEFUL DINING PHRASES

I would like a table for ... people
Je voudrais une table pour ... personnes
Zher voodray ewn tabl poor ... pehrson

Waiter/waitress!
Monsieur/Mademoiselle, s'il vous plaît!
M'sewr/madmwahzel, sylvooplay!

May I have the bill, please?
L'addition, s'il vous plaît!
Laddyssyawng, sylvooplay!

Could I have it well-cooked/medium/rare please?
Je le voudrais bien cuit/à point/ saignant
Zher ler voodray beeang kwee/ah pwang/saynyang

I am a vegetarian. Does this contain meat?
Je suis végétarien (végétarienne). Est-ce que ce plat contient de la viande?
Zher swee vehzhehtarianhg (vehzhehtarien). Essker ser plah kontyang der lah veeahngd?

Entertainment & nightlife

Outdoor entertainment

The nightlife of the city is pretty divided, with the Medina providing more traditional, and for the most part more sober, forms of entertainment, while Guéliz and the Palmeraie supply the majority of bars, clubs and discos. The Islamic rules of 'no alcohol' are not strictly enforced, especially for foreigners, but it's still easier to find drinks in the modern part of the city. The Jemaa el Fna is the centre

of traditional night entertainment, but there are more formal and touristy versions at the dinner shows just outside of town. The national symphony orchestra comes to town periodically and it's possible to hear them perform at the Opera/National Theatre. Cinema is very popular and it can be a real experience to join locals in their deck chairs in the open-air, watching the latest blockbusters.

The Medina's main focus of nightlife is at the Jemaa, with its

● *Orange juice sellers sustain the nightime crowds in the Jemaa*

varying forms of performance. The evening entertainment gradually evolves from the day's activities, although by about 18.00 most night events are beginning to happen. It's amazing to wander among the crowds, watching the storytellers, dancers, hawkers and musicians, and picking up some of the general energy of the place. If the hands-on experience is a bit too much, however, cafés and restaurants huddle around the square providing a somewhat distanced view of the activity. Most of these locales are multistorey, and higher floor or roof-top venues are always crowded.

Dinner shows can be pretty kitschy, idealising Moroccan culture and riding a bit heavy on the 'One Thousand and One Nights' mystique. However, it's worth attending just to watch the spectacular horsemanship of the recreated Fantasia. Presented at three venues outside of town:

Borj Bladi ❸ 57 rue Mauritania
Chez Ali ❸ Circuit Jaafaria
Kasbah Tassarout ❸ Route de Casablanca

Bars, clubs & casinos

Relatively few places within the Medina offer alcohol. Outside of the restaurants that serve wine with a meal, it's possible to get a drink at the (ironically named) Grand Hotel Tazi, a backpackers' hotel that has a cheap bar. On a more upmarket scale, the Jardins de la Kououbia, a large luxury hotel close to the Jemaa, has a place to sit and have a drink. The most impressive place to imbibe is the Churchill Piano Bar, located within the Hotel Mamounia grounds.

The new city, Guéliz, is much better stocked with bars. Many are located along the main boulevard, Mohammed V, and it's possible to get a drink here without any problem. In the nearby streets are other places as well, with both locals and visitors attending (and in many cases, accompanying trade). Discos are popular, most of them attached to hotels with predominantly foreign tourists. There are also some at Hivernage, an area of tourist development just west of the Medina walls. The Palmeraie, the trendiest location and a taxi drive away from the centre, is developing a reputation as a party place. Some of the more fashionable clubs are here.

Surprisingly, Marrakech also has a couple of casinos. The Grand Casino at the Hotel la Mamounia (❶ 044 38 86 00) has blackjack, craps and roulette. The one at the Es Saadi Hotel in Hivernage (❶ 044 44 88 11) is not quite as fancy, but will take your money just the same. Although neither charges an entry fee, minimum stakes are pretty high. Jacket and tie, and comparable attire for women, are required.

Music & cinema

The Moroccan Symphony Orchestra occasionally comes to Marrakech, but the best bet for music is still at the Jemaa. During the Popular Arts Festival in the city, or the Gnaoua Festival in Essaouria, it's possible to hear traditional musicians on a more formal basis.

Three cinemas in Guéliz and two in the Medina play the latest films, both from Hollywood and the rest of the world. However, the versions are dubbed in French and sometimes in Arabic. The Cinema Eden (❷ Derb Dabbach) is a concrete-floored venue with chairs set up for attendees. A party atmosphere pervades and here's a chance to get really close to the Marrakchi film fan base.

The Moroccan Tourist Board hasn't really got its listing act together, but a couple of guides come out at periodic intervals: *Marrakech Sejour & Loisirs*, sponsored by Royal Air Maroc, and *Marrakech Le magazine de la ville rouge*. The latter has a good website at ⓦ www.leguidemaroc.com.

Sport & relaxation

Even though Moroccans support football enthusiastically and Marrakech has a team in competition, active attendance is rare and most fans watch it at a distance. The city and its environs have their fair share of sporting and leisure activities, mostly due to the amenable climate that allows opportunities all year round. Hammams, or public baths, are a Moroccan institution and appear in many different guises.

SPECTATOR SPORTS
Football
Marrakchi prefer to support their teams by watching television with their mates, packed together in cafés. The resident soccer clubs, Kawkab and Najim, are based at the El Harti Stadium in Guéliz. When there's a game on, it's usually possible to buy tickets on the day. ⓐ Jnane el Harti, Guéliz ⓣ 044 42 06 66.

PARTICIPATION SPORTS
Golf
A very popular sport encouraged by reasonable green fees and international tournaments, there are three 18 hole courses:

Golf d'Amelkis ⓐ route de Ouarzazate ⓣ 044 40 44 14 ⓛ Daily 08.00–16.00 summer, 08.00–14.00 winter

Palmeraie Golf Palace ⓐ Hotel & Resort, Palmeraie ⓣ 044 30 110 10 ⓦ www.pgp.co.ma ⓛ Daily 07.00–19.00

Royal Golf Club ⓐ Ancienne route de Ouarzazate ⓣ 044 40 98 28 ⓛ Daily sunrise–sunset summer, 09.00–14.30 winter

Hiking
Although this takes place in the High Atlas, the city is a good place

to arrange excursions, if you haven't already done so. High Country
(Ⓦ www.highcountry.co.uk) and the Kasbah du Toubkal
(Ⓦ www.kasbahdutoubkal.com) can help plan hiking trips.

Karting & quad-biking

This sport has been soaring in popularity, with the semi-arid areas
around the city proving to be excellent grounds for roaring around.
Atlas Karting (ⓐ route de Safi Ⓣ 064 19 05 37) and Mega Quad
(ⓐ Tamesloht km 6, route d'Amizmiz Ⓣ 044 38 31 91), are two of the
best companies.

HAMMAMS

More of a social opportunity than a leisure activity, hammams
are public baths where the sexes are separated, and people
come to get clean.

The style and the quality of these baths may vary, but usually
there is a hot room where hot and cold water come from taps
and a bucket where the two can be mixed for pouring over the
body as required. In the next rooms are a cold water pool for a
quick bath and a space to cool down. Variations include
showers, and massages.

Although there are hammams all over the city, two of the
nicer ones are:

Hammam Ziani ⓐ 14 rue Riad Zitoune Ⓣ 062 71 55 71
Ⓛ Daily 07.00–22.30

La Maison Arabe ⓐ 1 Derb Assehbe, Bab Doukkala
Ⓣ 044 38 70 10 Ⓦ www.lamaisonarabe.com
Ⓛ by appointment

Horse riding

Partly due to royal patronage, equestrian sports are on the increase. One of the stables close to the centre is the Club Equestre de la Palmeraie ❸ Palmeraie Golf Palace Hotel & Resort, Palmeraie ❶ 044 36 87 93 Ⓦ www.pgp.co.ma Ⓒ Daily 08.00–12.00, 15.00–20.00 summer, 08.00–12.00, 15.00–18.00 winter.

Essaouira, 2.5 hours away from Marrakech, on the coast, offers horse and camel riding on the beach (see page 130).

Skiing

Seventy kilometres (43 miles) up the mountain in the High Atlas,

---

🔻 *Some of the best places for a little recreation are away from the city*

when there's snow at the winter resort of Oukaimeden, locals and tourists alike put on skis to use the chair lifts and downhill runs (see page 119).

Swimming

The best options for taking a dip are at the few hotels that have pools and allow visitors to use the facilities for a fee:

Palmeraie Golf Palace (see page 47) ⓐ Palmeraie ⓣ 044 36 87 93

Sheraton ⓐ avenue de la Menara, Hivernage ⓣ 044 44 89 98.

Nikki Beach Club in the Palmeraie is a branch of the chain that offers swimming and club facilities for day use. Cocktails are also served. ⓐ Circuit de la Palmeraie ⓣ 044 36 87 27 ⓦ www.nikkibeach.com.

Accommodation

There are a phenomenal number of places to stay in the city, ranging from a campsite and youth hostel to some of the finest hotels in the world. In between are *riads*, a sort of boutique bed & breakfast-cum-guesthouse-cum-hotel virtually unique to Marrakech. Mostly in the Medina, these places are often unmarked and hidden, frequently requiring a walk through labyrinthine streets too narrow for cars. Originally private houses with courtyards, the residences were bought up, decorated and furnished to the purchasers' tastes. Quite a few have been acquired by Europeans, some who intended to move in and live full time, others who were looking for holiday or investment opportunities. As Marrakech began to become a fashionable tourist destination, these owners realised that they could rent out rooms and recover some of their costs. There are now over 400 *riads*, all with a relatively small number of rooms, and each a unique assembly of personal taste. Some of them are absolutely exquisite – with prices to match – and some are remarkably good value. There are even a few with swimming pools, although the restrictions of space within the cramped Medina make this a rarity. They all include breakfast, many offering beverages or afternoon snacks. Most can also arrange an evening meal, either cooked on site or brought in from a local restaurant, effectively acting as room service. European-owned residences often provide alcohol. What proves to be a problem with *riads* is the same thing that makes them so desirable – their small size. The more popular ones soon fill up, so booking ahead is often essential.

Decent alternatives do exist, and there are some excellent hotels in Marrakech. The most famous, the Mamounia, is a world in itself. Within the new city, the hotel chains, such as Ibis and Sofitel, are

PRICE RATING

The bigger hotels conform to a star, and the smaller hotels to a lantern, rating system, but as so many places to stay are individually owned, the designations have little comparative value. Prices for a single night in a double room for two persons are:

D = up to D800   **DD** = D800–D2000   **DDD**= over D2000

well represented. Medium-level hotels are also in Guéliz, for those visitors looking for something halfway between small *riads* and enormous hotels. Beyond, in the Palmeraie, are huge hotel resorts that are quite a distance away from the Medina, but offer full sport and leisure facilities as recompense.

If travelling independently, deciding where to stay can be difficult. The choices listed on the following pages are by necessity subjective and only a tiny selection. For more information check out the following websites: **Hotels & Riads** Ⓦ www.riadsmorocco.com; **Special Places to Stay** Ⓦ www.specialplacestostay.com; ilove-marrakech Ⓦ www.ilove-marrakech.com; and **The Best of Morocco**, Ⓦ www.morocco-travel.com.

HOTELS & RIADS

Hotel Ali D Popular with backpackers, this cheap and cheerful hotel is centrally situated and has a bureau de change and internet café. ⓐ rue Moulay Ismail, Medina ❶ 044 44 49 79.

CTM D Although a little rough, this hotel is inexpensive and has a great location on the main square. ⓐ Jemaa el Fna Medina ❶ 044 44 23 25.

Dar Fakir D This newly converted *riad* is beautifully furnished with large full-facility rooms. ❷ 16 Derb Abou el Fadall Medina ❶ 044 44 11 00.

Grand Hotel Tazi D Hardly grand, this is one of the cheaper places to stay in the Medina. It's popular with backpackers, not just because of the price, but also because of the bar serving cheap beer. ❷ Angle Av. El Mouahidine et Rue Bab Agnaou, Medina ❶ 044 44 27 87.

Hotel Ibis D Part of the economy branch of the Accor chain, this hotel is surprisingly nice, with a large pool, situated right next to the railway station. ❷ Avenue Hassan II, Place de la Gare, Guéliz ❶ 044 43 59 29 33 ❿ www.accorhotels.com

Hotel Islane D An inexpensive hotel located directly across from the Koutoubia minaret; a good restaurant and excellent ice cream stand are on the premises. ❷ 279 Avenue Med. V, Medina ❶ 044 44 00 81.

Hotel Sherazade D One of the best-value small hotels in the Medina, the décor is simple but friendly. ❷ Derb Djama 3 t Riad Zitoun L´Kedim, Medina ❶ 044 42 93 05 ❿ www.hotelsherazade.com

Morocco House Hotel D (for 3 star) Located in the middle of the new city, this friendly, comfortable, hotel gives its guests a choice of 3-, 4- or 5-star accommodation. ❷ 3 Rue Loubnane, Guéliz ❶ 044 42 03 05 ❿ www.moroccanhousehotels.com

La Maison Arabe DD One of Marrakech's finest, and best-known small hotels, the restaurant – and cookery school – are also famous.

● *Each riad – Moroccan boutique hotel – has its own character*

● 1 Derb Assehbe, Bab Doukkala, Medina ● 044 38 70 10
Ⓦ www.lamaisonarabe.com

Maison Mnabha DD This lovely *riad* in the Kasbah area of the
Medina is English owned and run, yet still a Maison de Charme.
● 32–33 Derb Mnabha, Kasbah, Medina ● 044 38 13 25
Ⓦ www.maisonmnabha.com

Riad 72 DD The unique appeal of this *riad* is its lovely Italian-Moroccan design mix. It's located in the Medina, north of the Jemaa. ⓐ 72 Arset Awsel, Bab Doukkala, Medina ⓣ 044 38 76 29 ⓦ www.riad72.com

Riyad el Cadi DD Appearing to be more a gallery than a residence, this opulent houaw was once the home of the fine art collecting German ambassador to Morocco ⓐ 87 Derb Moulay Abdul Kader, Derb Dabachi, Medina ⓣ 044 37 86 55 ⓦ www.riyadelcadi.com

Riad Magi DD Huddled around a delightful central courtyard, this *riad* has some intriguing design features. The English owners of this charming place are wonderfully friendly and incredibly helpful. ⓐ 79 Derb Moulay Abdul Kader, Derb Dabachi, Medina ⓣ 044 42 68 88

Sofitel DD Up to its usual luxury hotel standard, the top link of the Accor chain has a large presence just outside the Medina. ⓐ Rue Harroun Errachid, Hivernage ⓣ 044 42 56 00 ⓦ www.accorhotels.com

Hotel Mamounia DDD The Grand-dame of Marrakech, this fabulous, if somewhat exclusive, hotel still has the glamorous aura of its art deco era (see page 73). ⓐ Avenue Bab Jdid, Medina ⓣ 044 38 86 00 ⓦ www.mamounia.com

Janane Tamsna DDD An exquisite *riad*-like hotel that has already developed legendary status for its stunning design and incredible décor. ⓐ Palmeraie (phone for directions) ⓣ 044 32 94 23 ⓦ www.tamsna.com

Jardins de la Koutoubia DDD Despite being right off the main square, this large modern deluxe hotel with huge pool is surprisingly quiet. ⓐ 26 rue de la Koutoubia ⓣ 044 38 88 00 ⓦ www.lesjardinsdelakoutoubia.com/anglais

Jardins de la Medina DDD This first-class luxurious accommodation is tucked away in the Kasbah area of the Medina. ⓐ 21 Derb Chtouka, Kasbah, Medina ⓣ 044 38 18 51 ⓦ www.lesjardinsdelamedina.com

La Villa des Orangers DDD Another wonderful, luxurious secret hiding right behind the main square, the only Relais & Chateaux-rated hotel in Morocco also has a pool. ⓐ rue Sidi Mimoun, Medina ⓣ 044 38 46 38 ⓦ www.villadesorangers.com

Palmeraie Golf Palace DDD An enormous complex just outside Marrakech includes an 18-hole golf course, horse riding, swimming pools (see page 41) and a luxury hotel. ⓐ Les Jardins de la Palmeraie BP: 1488 ⓣ 044 30 50 50 ⓦ www.pgp.co.ma

HOSTELS & CAMPSITES
Auberge de jeunesse The Marrakech youth hostel is located outside the Medina, in the Hivernage area of town. ⓐ Rue El Jahed, Quartier Industriel, Hivernage ⓣ 044 44 77 13.

Camping Ferdaous Marrakech's campsite is a bit far from the centre although close to the Marjane Hypermarket. ⓐ 13 km Carretera Casablanca ⓣ 024 31 31 67.

THE BEST OF MARRAKECH

Whether you are on a flying visit to Marrakech or have a little more time to explore the city and its surroundings, there are some sights, places and experiences that you should not miss. For the best attractions for children, see pages 147–148.

TOP 10 ATTRACTIONS

- **Koutoubia** Marrakech's landmark is a graceful 12th-century minaret towering 77 m (252 ft) above the city (see page 76).

- **Jemaa el Fna** This huge square has Moroccan street entertainment during the day and – even better – at night (see page 73).

- **Souks** The inner city's markets are fabulous to look at as well as excellent places to buy a remarkable array of goods (see page 79).

- **Bahia Palace** A beautiful 19th-century palace filled with courtyards, gardens and exquisite detailing (see page 66).

▼ *Painted ceilings and wooden carvings enhance the Bahia Palace*

- **El Badi** The ruins of an enormous royal residence of the late 16th century, this massive space has an awesome ambience (see page 71).

- **Saadian tombs** Graves of the dynasty's princes are situated in lovely gardens, enhanced by beautiful Moroccan representational art (see page 79).

- **Ben Youssef Medersa** Once a Koranic school, these courtyards flanked by what were once students' cells are full of magnificent examples of Hispano-Moorish decoration (see page 68).

- **City Gates** The ancient entry points into the Medina through the city walls still have the power to impress (see page 71).

- **Majorelle Gardens** Literally an oasis in the new town, the eponymous artist's lush exotic gardens were restored by the fashion designer, Yves Saint-Laurent (see page 98).

- **Hotel Mamounia** An art deco palace, it's worth saving up some pennies and dressing up a bit and for afternoon tea at this 1920s architectural institution. (see page 73).

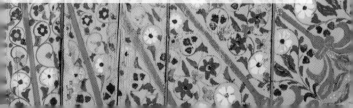

Your brief guide to seeing the best that Marrakech has to offer, depending on how much time you have.

HALF-DAY: MARRAKECH IN A HURRY

Start at the Koutoubia, then wander a bit further to explore the gardens that are close to the base of the tower. Turn back towards the Jemaa el Fna and spend some time watching the snake charmers, monkey dancers and weird herbal salesmen. Don't forget to try some orange juice from any of the many vendors. Head north into the maze of souks and just wander, letting whim take hold. If the opportunity allows, drop in and visit the Bahia Palace. Save a little time for a stop at a café in order to try a mint tea.

1 DAY: TIME TO SEE A LITTLE MORE

With a few more hours available, spend more time in the souks, perhaps ambling towards the smaller alleyways and backstreets to watch the craftsmen working. Continue north to visit the Ben Youssef Medersa, buying the combined ticket that allows entry to the nearby Qoubba and Marrakech Museum. While at the Medersa, make sure you go upstairs to see a few of the cells. Continue across the way to the impressive remains of the Qoubba, the washing pool of the Almoravid, and the only building left from that period. The Marrakech Museum has a delightful outdoor café to enjoy a coffee, or perhaps another mint tea. Alternatively, head towards the nearest taxi for a ride up to the Majorelle Gardens. Spend the evening at the Jemaa el Fna, listening to the (Arabic) storytellers and musicians.

2–3 DAYS: SHORT CITY BREAK

Take advantage of the extra time to visit some more sights, such as the Badi Palace ruins and the Saadian tombs. With a day or two more, it's possible to view some museums, including the Dar Si Said's assembly of fine Moroccan decorative art, or Maison Tiskiwin, holding the private stash of the Dutch art collector, Bert Flint. Sit back in the seat of a horse-drawn *caléche* while circling the city walls. In late afternoon, dress up and stop at the Mamounia, using the excuse of a cup of tea to view the grounds and gardens.

LONGER: ENJOYING MARRAKECH TO THE FULL

If it's possible to get away from browsing and shopping in the souks, or watching the continually changing entertainment at the Jemaa, a day or more away from the city shows off an entirely different side of Morocco. There are numerous possibilities for excursions into the High Atlas Mountains, ranging from visiting a truly rural weekly market, to ascending the tallest mountain in North Africa. Another option for a few days is to head towards the seaside, particularly the charming and laid-back fishing village of Essaouira. With its long, wide beach and excellent windsurfing environment, but without the development and tourism of Agadir, this artist's haven is a delightful break from the energy of Marrakech.

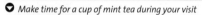

Make time for a cup of mint tea during your visit

Something for nothing

Marrakech is not an expensive city and most entry fees to museums are pretty low. Nevertheless, if looking after every single dirham is an issue, then there are several options for free things to do.

Most interesting is the entertainment in the Jemaa el Fna, for which there is no charge. Of course, the performers work for tips, but these are not mandatory. Storytellers, who don't speak in French or English anyway, will begin their tales and stop when they reach a critical point. Here, they will ask for an onlooker to give some money to continue, and generally someone does. Musicians and dancers

● *They don't charge, but musicians in the Jemaa will expect a tip*

work the crowd and all are invited to watch. It's possible to have a fascinating evening, or even an interesting day here, without spending a penny.

Further within the Medina are the souks that seem to extend endlessly. When the markets appear to come to an end, they start again a bit further on, so that 'window shopping' is an activity that can easily take all day. Sometimes it's possible to witness the creation of the goods, seeing how wool is dyed in the Souk Sebbaghine, or watching leather goods being stitched in the Souk Cherratine. It's always fun to watch tourists bargaining with the stallholders, and quite possibly a good opportunity to pick up some negotiating tips, although try to avoid the groups who travel en masse.

The gardens outside the city walls are open to the public at no charge, and are well attended. The Koutoubia Gardens have roses for most of the year and are pleasant to walk through, although sometimes a little unkempt. A little further along is the Cyber Parc, lovely well manicured gardens that are dotted with computer terminals. With the purchase of a phone card, it's possible to make economical phone calls here, or even go online pretty cheaply. The bright Moroccan sunshine often means it's difficult to see the screen, but the locals seem to use the machines in any weather. The other well-known green spaces are a bit further away, and require either quite a long walk or a short taxi ride. The Menara Gardens are quite historic and have a large pond with a famous pavilion on its edge. A bit characterless and barren, this place is best outside of the summer, when the air is clear and the often snow-covered Atlas Mountains are reflected in the water. The Agdal Gardens belong to the Royal Palace Grounds, and parts of it are open on Fridays and Sundays. Locals love to take along their stale bread and feed the ravenous – and increasingly large – carp in the reservoir.

When it rains

Wet weather can create havoc, turning unpaved roads into muddy slush, and slowing traffic down into a dirty mess. It's not usually a problem, though, as rain falls mostly in the winter, and even then, the average is barely more than a couple of centimetres per month. Unfortunately, it tends to come down all at once, so it's probably wise to hide out if the sky begins to turn dark grey.

The best places to take refuge while still enjoying the sights are the museums. The Dar Si Said in the Medina is in a beautifully preserved palace, and comprises the South Morocco Regional Arts Museum. A quick dash away is the Dar Tiskiwin and the contents, Moroccan traditional art, are inside the house of the owner. Not far away is the Lazama synagogue, and it's possible to visit it in the rain, although by the time you find your way there, through the twists and turns of the Jewish Mellah, you might already be soaked (it's best to request directions from a local and accept that, by asking, you're hiring an unofficial guide). Further north is the Marrakech Museum, a large rambling palace that has lots of rooms and various permanent and visiting exhibitions. If the rain isn't too bad, it might be worth taking in the Ben Youssef Medersa nearby, as much of it is covered. Some of the private galleries such as La Quobba Galerie in the Medina, or La Galerie Bleu in Guéliz, have the work of contemporary Moroccan artists, which makes a change from seeing all that 'old stuff'.

Bad weather might provide an excellent chance to try the hammams. Located at various places throughout the city, and available in all shapes and sizes (and prices), wallowing in a bathhouse is a very Moroccan thing to do. Add a massage to complete the experience.

Having a cup of coffee, or sipping yet another mint tea, can also be a way of taking shelter on a wet day. Some of the nicer places, such as Dar Timtam, Riad Tamsna, and even the Hotel Mamounia, have areas where afternoon refreshment is served inside, in an extremely picturesque environment. Otherwise, some of the more basic cafés, such as those surrounding the Jemaa el Fna, still give some sort of cover, while providing an opportunity for some great people-watching.

⬤ *It doesn't rain often, but you can always head inside the Marrakech Museum*

On arrival

TIME DIFFERENCES

Marrakech is on Greenwich Mean Time (GMT) all year round. When it is 12.00 noon in the Moroccan summer, time at home is as follows:

Australia Eastern Standard Time 22.00, Central Standard Time 21.30, Western Standard Time 20.00
South Africa 14.00
New Zealand 22.00
UK 13.00
USA and Canada Newfoundland Time 09.30, Atlantic Canada Time 09.00, Eastern Time 07.00, Central Time 06.00, Mountain Time 05.00, Pacific Time 04.00, Alaska 03.00.

ARRIVING

The most convenient way to get to Marrakech for a short break is to fly, and planes land at the Aeroport Marrakech Menara, very close to the city centre. With a bit more time, travelling by train is an option, and although only domestic routes travel through Morocco, it's possible to make the relevant connection for the south just after the ferry port, at Tangier. As for driving, the fastest way from Europe is to cross the Straits of Gibraltar, head west towards Casablanca then south to Marrakech.

By air

Marrakech Menara Airport (❶ 044 44 79 10), is a mere 6 km (4 miles) west of the city centre. As the airport is small, there are not many facilities here. A couple of banks provide currency exchange.

Buses and taxis drive into the city, or possibly a bit further, depending on where you want to end up. The local no. 11 bus stop is just outside the airport and it goes directly to the Jemaa el Fna. It's very cheap, and runs about every 20 minutes during the week, and at longer intervals on weekends.

Taxis are either the shared 'Grands' or individual 'petit'. The former are more likely to be around, and, although effectively paying for six people, prices are quite reasonable. There are meters, but drivers are often hesitant to use them. It's best to agree on a price beforehand, but it shouldn't be much than 60–70 dirham. If any are available and there are not more than two passengers, a smaller 'petit' taxi, is slightly cheaper. Bear in mind, if you are travelling away from the city itself, that petit taxis cannot drive beyond the city limits.

By rail

The city's rail station (ⓐ avenue Hassan II ① 044 44 77) is housed in a charming, colonial-style building in Guéliz. As Marrakech is the end of the line, passenger traffic is fairly high for such a small terminus. It's possible to travel all over Morocco from here, although changes might be necessary. It's advisable to travel first class which is not much more expensive than second class, and, in itself, fairly cheap. The rail system is the ONCF, and their online timetable is ⓦ www.oncf.ma.

By bus

Long-distance buses are by far the least expensive way to travel across Morocco, although they take much longer than planes or trains. For destinations close to Marrakech, such as Essaouira, they are a cheaper option than taxis.

The main bus station (📍 Place El Mouarabitène, Bab Doukkala ☎ 044 43 39 33) can be a bit chaotic. The Guéliz departure point may be a bit easier to handle (📍 12 boulevard Zerktouni ☎ 044 44 83 28).

DRIVING

Although driving within the city is neither necessary nor recommended, it can be useful to have a car when exploring the rest of Morocco. A motorway links Tangier and Casablanca, and a decent road, of which about a quarter of the way is autoroute, completes the trip to Marrakech. Once in the city, however, parking is difficult. If staying in the Medina, take your chances and leave the car at a pay lot, near the city wall. Alternatively, choose a hotel that has a large parking area, such as in Guéliz or the Palmeraie.

FINDING YOUR FEET

There are two distinct aspects of Marrakech, the old city, Medina, and the new, Guéliz. The Medina is where tourists spend most of their time. Surrounded by intact walls, there are various gates through which one enters, some wide enough for cars and others for foot traffic only. Some of the bigger roads around the edges can support motor vehicles but, in general, the Medina is a pedestrian area. Horse-drawn *calèches*, motor scooters, donkey carts and bicycles are exceptions, but that doesn't mean there is actually enough room – watch out for them when wandering through some of the major thoroughfares. Guéliz is big and modern, with large boulevards and a great deal of motor traffic. Overall, Marrakech is pretty safe, adhering to the rules of respect inherent in Muslim tradition. Nevertheless, as with any country where there is a wide

● *Hitting the bustling streets of Marrakech may bring on culture shock*

French Cultural Institute

Palmeraie

Museum of Islamic Arts ■

Majorelle
Gardens

Manso

Av. Yacoub El

Boulevard de Safi

Blvd. Mohamed V

Zerktouni

Bd. Mohamed

Rue de Liberté

GUÉLIZ

Avenue de France

Bd Moulay Rachid

Place du 16
Novembre

Av. des Nations Unie

Blvd. Mohamed V

Rail
Station ■

Avenue Hassan II

Av. Yacoub El Marini

Place de la
Liberté

Opera ■

Rue El Oadr Ayad

Rue Jaber Ben Hayane

Blvd El Yarr

Palais de
Congres ■

Avenue Moulay El Hassan

Route de la Piscine

Avenue de France

Av. du Pres Kennedy

R

Avenue de la Ménara

Menara
Gardens

Airport ↓

City Walls

les Remparts

on
**Zaouia Sidi
Ben Slimane**

Rue El Gza

Rue de Bab Tagghzout

Rue As Ouel

Route des Remparts

Rue de Bab El Khémis

Ben Youssef Mosque

Rue de Bab Doukkala

Rue du Bab Debbarh

City Walls

Marrakech Museum

Rue Fatima Zohra

Kissaria

**La Criée
Berbere**

MEDINA

R. de Bab Ailen

isemble
rtisinal

Rue Sidi El Yamami

R. Derb Dabachi

R. de Bab Aghmat

oti   Blvd. Mohammed V

Jemaa
El Fna

Rue Riad Zitoun el Kedim

Rue Riad Zitoun el Jdid

Rue Douar Graoua

oubia
que

**Dar Si Said
Musée d'art
Régional**

Umman El Fetouaki

**Dar
Tiskiwin**

lotel
imounia

Av. Oumman El Fetouaki

Rue Imam El Rhazali

Bahia Palace

**Bab
Agnaou**

Kasbah Mosque

MELLAH

Saadian Tombs

City Walls

Rue de la Kasba

El Badi Palais

Royal Palace

Agdal Gardens

0   500m

N

gap between rich and poor, don't flaunt items of value unnecessarily. It's also advisable to dress respectfully, especially for women. Keep shoulders covered, and wear trousers or long skirts, rather than shorts, at least in the Medina.

ORIENTATION

A huge ochre wall surrounds the historic centre completely and is a useful way of recognising the line between the old (Medina) and new (Guéliz) areas of the city. The focal point of the Medina is the main square, the Jemaa el Fna, which is directly across from the Koutoubia, the tall minaret that is visible from almost any open space. If lost, just ask for the Jemaa, and most people will be able to offer directions. The souk area is to the north of the main square.

To the south are some of the most important attractions, and past the Badi is the Royal Palace. On the extended grounds of this regal residence are the Agdal Gardens.

To the west of the Jemaa is the Mamounia Hotel, just inside the city walls, and beyond are the Hivernage and southern side of Guéliz. Boulevard Mohammed V straddles the division between the two sections of the city, and goes past the Place du 16 Novembre to the Abd el Moumen Ben Ali Square, the heart of the modern city.

GETTING AROUND

Wandering around the Medina is best done on foot. It may be possible to rent a bicycle, but with the density of the crowds this form of transport isn't recommended. If walking proves too exhausting, hiring a horse-drawn *calèche* is an option, and the drivers will take chances that non-residents never would, but even they are restricted by their carriages' width.

Taxis can be found at the limits of their range, e.g. at the Jemaa, or around the city gates. They are plentiful, reasonably priced and extremely convenient. In a pale yellow shade for Marrakech (other regions have different colours), they come in two sizes, 'petit' (small) and 'grand'. The petit taxis are small cars, holding a maximum of three passengers, and are available for individual fares. The grand taxis, usually Mercedes, are meant for up to six people, and will charge accordingly. In some cases, the bigger taxis will stop for other passengers en route in order to fill their cabs. Sometimes the meter will run and sometimes not, and prices are usually negotiable ahead of time. Late in the evening fares go up.

Buses run between the old and new cities. They can save quite a lot of walking, as the distances between the two parts of town can be pretty large. The fares are low but the buses can also get very crowded. Make sure you have small change, as the driver never does. Route no. 1 runs along blvd Mohammed V, from the Jemaa el Fna to Guéliz.

IF YOU GET LOST, TRY ...

Excuse me, is this the right way to the tourist office/ the bus station?
Excusez-moi, c'est la bonne direction pour l'office de tourisme/la gare routière?
Ekskewzaymwah, seh lah bon deerekseeawng poor lohfeece de tooreezm/lah gahr rootyair?

Can you point to it on my map?
Pouvez-vous me le montrer sur la carte?
Poovehvoo mer ler mawngtreh sewr lah kart?

CAR HIRE

There is no need to have your own transport for a city break in Marrakech. Even for short excursions to destinations nearby, hiring a taxi for a day or two is probably cheaper than renting a car. If you are planning an extended visit to places further away, hiring a vehicle is an option, although it's relatively expensive to do so. The smallest economy car's daily fee, with unlimited mileage and insurance, costs around 1000 dirhams, with a medium-sized vehicle priced around 2140 dirhams. Weekly rates are lower pro rata, with the same cars costing 3300 dirhams and 7600 dirhams. It's best to stick with the larger, better-known rental companies, as they are more reliable, and their insurance coverage guaranteed. Better deals might be found by booking an automobile as part of a fly-drive package.

Avis ☎ 044 43 25 25 Ⓦ www.avis.ma
Budget ☎ airport: 044 43 88 75; Guéliz: 044 43 11 80
Ⓦ www.budget.com
Europcar ☎ 022 31 37 37
Ⓦ www.1stmaroc.com/europcar/europcar.html
Hertz ☎ airport: 044 44 72 30; Guéliz: 044 43 99 84
Ⓦ www.hertz.co.uk
Thrifty ☎ 061 80 69 63 Ⓦ www.thrifty-maroc.ma

● *Non-stop Jemaa el Fna in the Medina is the heart of the city*

THE CITY OF
Marrakech

The Medina

Most of Marrakech's tourist attractions are located within the Medina. Surrounded by walls that are worth a look in their own right, the ancient city contains the Jemaa el Fna (the central square), monuments, mosques, museums, palaces and tombs that are what visitors come to see. The souks, the typical markets, seem to go on endlessly with their phenomenal array of goods, and are probably the best in North Africa.

Street cafés are everywhere, and sipping mint tea or coffee in an open square or exclusive private *riad* is a great way to take a break. There are restaurants ranging from casual locales to fine gourmet venues with excellent views. Beginning at dusk, the Jemaa has dozens of stalls where food is selected, prepared and served right in front of its customers. The main square is where the majority of the Medina's entertainment is based, during both day and night, although it's possible to catch a movie at the local cinema.

SIGHTS & ATTRACTIONS

Almoravid Qoubba

This unassuming domed ablutions pool is the only structure left from the period of the Almoravids (early 12th century). Unimpressive from a distance, once inside, the ancient fountain is simple yet nicely decorated. ❷ place Ben Youssef/Kissaria ❶ 044 39 09 11 ❶ daily 09.00–16.00.

Bahia Palace

Hidden behind high walls that insulate the grounds from noise, as well as the outside world, this magnificent palace was the residence

of Ba Ahmed Ben Moussa, a grand vizier in the 19th century. Built for his four wives, 24 concubines and their brood, the complex is a sequence of courtyards, fountains and chambers. Exquisitely enhanced with painted ceilings, fine stucco detailing and carved wood, the palace presents excellent examples of period interior decoration and is a delightful place to linger. ❷ Riad Zitoun Jihad ❶ 044 38 92 21 ● Sat–Thur 08.00–11.45, 14.00–17.45, Fri 08.00–11.30, 15.00–17.45.

Ben Youssef Medersa
Built as a Koranic school in the 16th century, the Medersa is a series of simple, monastic-like student rooms, surrounding a large central courtyard. The pool in the centre is made from Carrara marble, which glows white in the bright sunshine. The common areas, like the prayer rooms and classrooms, are magnificently decorated with incredibly elaborate carvings in stucco and wood. A stunning example of Moorish architecture and design. ❸ Place Ben Youssef/Kissaria ❶ 044 39 09 11 ● Daily 09.00–18.00.

City Walls
Enclosing the Medina, these 10 m (33 ft) high walls follow the original 12th-century ramparts built by the Sultan Ali Ben Youssef. Still constructed from pisé (mud and clay mixed with straw and lime), they run the 10 km (6 mile) circumference around the city. The best way to view their entirety is by horse-drawn *calèches*, as on the route are areas of not much interest to the pedestrian. The stretch at the Medina entrance leading from the Avenue de la Menara is particularly dramatic.

● *High walls separate the old city (the Medina) from the newer areas*

A WALK IN THE MEDINA – PALACES

Begin at the Jemaa el Fna with the Koutoubia mosque behind you. Cross the square, then turn right into the Rue Riad Zitoun el Kdim. Follow this bigger street south to the Place Qzadria. En route, wander into the side passages, getting a glimpse into some of Marrakech's real life. Seemingly confusing, the little streets will eventually take the pedestrian to a larger thoroughfare that runs parallel and will lead again to the Place. Don't be afraid to get lost – all routes eventually get through and the locals can always give directions to the major tourist sites. On arrival, cross over to the Place des Ferblantiers and take a look at the beautiful lamps, candlelabra and other items crafted in metal. Opposite the square is the treasure chest of the Sagha, the small arcade stuffed full of gold jewellery stores. The Qzadria Square is a good central location. Heading east will lead to the beautiful 19th-century Bahia Palace. Across from here is the Mellah, the Jewish quarter, in which is located the old synagogue. More confusing to explore than it appears on maps, it's advisable to accept the offers of the locals to show you around (for a tip, of course). Immediately south of Qzadria Square are the impressive remains of the Badi Palace. Continuing in the same direction leads to the Royal Palace, and the Agdal Gardens beyond. Back to the square, head west to the entryway of the Kasbah. Turn left alongside the city walls, then left again near the enormous Bab Agnaou city gate, to take you past the magnificent Kasbah mosque. Just beyond is the entrance to the Saadian tombs. Retrace your steps to get back to the Jemaa.

City Gates (Babs)

Puncturing the relatively featureless walls are the 19 City Gates. Located all around the Medina, some of these entrances are magnificent gateways while others are simply modern access points. Baba Agnaou and the Royal Palace's Bab Ighlil to the southwest are two of the more impressive portals.

Debbaghine

The tanners' district is far to the east of the Medina and well away from the noses of most tourists. Here is where the animal skins are tanned and treated to become the material for the goods in the leather market. Large pits are dug into the ground and filled with lime, tannin and pigeon dung, the chemical combination used for preparation. The smell is awful, and this vision of hell is only visible from nearby rooftops, but the leather does come out remarkably supple.

El Badi Palace

The large ruins of El Badi still give off an aura of wealth and power. Once 'incomparable', the lavish 16th-century palace of Ahmed El Mansour was so legendary that the next century's Alaouite dynasty's Sultan Moulay Ismail took a full ten years to strip it of its luxurious materials. Today, it's quite peaceful strolling around the vast concrete grounds with what remains of the walls. From the upper levels there is a spectacular view of the High Atlas Mountains on clear days. On display in the exhibition area in the back is the 17th-century wooden minbar (pulpit) taken from the Koutoubia.

The storks resting on their gigantic nests, perched on the corners of the top floors, are also fun to watch. The open-air Badi palace is still used for Marrakech's major events, the Festival of Popular Arts

held in June, and the International Film Festival in November.
🕐 Daily 08.00–12.00, 14.00–18.30.

🔺 *Follow in the footsteps of a statesmen at the Mamounia's Churchill suite*

Hotel Mamounia

Marrakech's legendary hotel (see accommodation page 46) is a tourist attraction and worth a visit, even if you're not staying or eating here. Exemplary of its 1920s art deco period, the interior decoration has been beautifully maintained. The Imperial Restaurant has a ceiling painted by the artist Majorelle (see page 98), and the suite that Winston Churchill occupied when a regular visitor to what he considered 'the most beautiful place in the world' has been preserved. The extensive gardens – 20 acres of them – full of orange trees and date palms, are surprisingly peaceful considering their proximity to traffic. If not a guest, a dress code is strictly enforced – make sure to wear the best clothes you have with you, as 'bouncers' at the door will refuse entry to non-residents dressed in jeans and hiking boots. Be warned: the prices for most things – including a cup of tea – can seem incredibly high.

ⓐ Avenue Bab Jdid, Medina ⓣ 044 38 86 00 ⓦ www.mamounia.com

Jemaa el Fna

This large open space is the Medina's centre, in spirit rather than in geography. Everything leads back to this square and it's always a handy reference point in coming or going. It lies next to the Koutoubia minaret and alongside Mohammed V, the major urban thoroughfare of Marrakech.

Originally part of the Almoravid royal residence, the land reverted to a public area when the next dynasty, the Almohads, moved the palace to a different location. Also the spot where execution victims were put on display, the square became known as the Jemaa el Fna: the 'gathering place of the dead'. The name has stuck even after the bodies were cleared away, and the place is now known as 'the J'ma'.

Ironically, the square is the liveliest place in Marrakech. Designated as a 'Heritage of Humanity' site by UNESCO, the Jemaa is host to myriad activities, many distinctly ethnic. During the day it's possible to find traditional medicine sellers with their weird wares spread put on the ground, teeth pullers surrounded by their conquests, snake charmers and their menagerie of reptiles and dancing monkeys. At night, the animals are put away and replaced by more human activities, such as the telling of stories (see page 76), tumbling by acrobats, dancing by transvestites and the playing of music on traditional instruments. Crowds gather around each performer and the square gets so busy it's almost impossible to cross. The atmosphere is electric with everyone out to have a good time.

Orange juice and dried fruit and nuts salesmen are at the square all hours, but at dusk the food stalls are brought in. Huddled together with narrow rows between them, each displays its wares, offering to cook to order. Hawkers accost the visitors, promising their food is the best. The eateries are licensed, and have numbers displayed at the top to prove it. However, they are not laid out in numerical order, and it can be difficult to find any particular one, in the case of a previous recommendation. It's simpler to judge a place on how the food looks as well as the number of locals who are eating there.

Kasbah

This area of the Medina is the most complete urban Kasbah (defined as: the citadel, or quarter in which the citadel is located) in Morocco. It was built in the 12th century to house the servants and employees attendant to the Almohad Royal Palace, once located just to the south. The construction extended the city boundaries. One of the most impressive gates in the original wall, the Bab Agnaou, is the entryway through which one enters the Kasbah. Dominated by

⬥ *Not everyone is charmed by this fascinating Marrakchi tradition*

the beautiful minaret of the Kasbah mosque, the enclave has a 'city within a city' feel. The Saadian Tombs are located here.

STORYTELLERS OF THE JEMAA

The storytellers of Marrakech's main square, the Jemaa el Fna, are one of the main reasons that UNESCO has designated this area as a humanity heritage site. Important exponents of the oral tradition, these tellers of tales always manage to gather huge crowds around them. Speaking in Arabic, they cater their accounts to locals rather than tourists. The storyteller begins his tale, building up the tension – and just as he comes to a critical point, stops. At this stage, the speaker will ask the audience if anyone is willing to pay him to continue. Inevitably, someone rises from the group, hands the teller a coin, and the man continues with his story. As the evening progresses, so does the tale, with the listeners eventually getting the whole account, and the storyteller earning his keep.

Koutoubia

Marrakech's icon is the minaret of the Koutoubia ('booksellers') mosque, named after the businesses that once thrived at its base. Built in the 12th century in a Hispano-Moorish style similar to its cousin, the Giralda in Seville, its dimensions of 1:5, width to height, make the tower slim and graceful. The mosque to which the Koutoubia belongs is not accessible to non-Muslims, but the square next to it, and the adjoining rose gardens, are open to the public.
☎ 044 43 26 39.

▶ *The minaret of a mosque – the Koutoubia – forms the city's landmark*

Mellah

The Jewish quarter of the Medina is a ghost of what it used to be, as most of the members of the once-large ethnic population left in the mid- to late 20th century. The narrow winding streets are run-down and of little interest to tourists.

Within the district remains the ancient Lazama Synagogue. Originally constructed in the 16th century when the Jews were an important part of the commercial life of the Medina, it's now the oldest one left in the city. If you can find your way there, tours are offered by the resident custodian. A large but unimpressive Jewish cemetery lies to the east.

Also in the Mellah is a small, unassuming covered market selling spices and basics. Nearby is the Sagha, the Marché des Bijouterie, or gold market. Located discreetly within a small arcade, the shop windows are stuffed full of gold trinkets. Lazama Synagogue
ⓐ Derb Manchoura ⓒ Daily 09.00–18.00.

Mosques

Even though Marrakech's mosques are not open to non-Muslims, the buildings are still an important part of the cityscape. The exteriors are dramatic and often quite beautiful, with the tall minarets not only typical examples of period architecture, but also excellent landmarks by which to find your way through the Medina. The call to prayer, broadcast five times a day, gets to be a familiar sound.

A few of the more outstanding mosques are:

Koutoubia ⓐ nr Mohammed V

Bab Doukkala ⓐ rue Bab Doukkala

Ben Youssef ⓐ near the Medersa at Place Ben Youssef/Kissaria

Kasbah ⓐ rue de la Kasbah .

Saadian Tombs

Hidden away under the shadow of the Kasbah mosque is a discreet entrance that leads through a series of passages. At the end is a large garden, with open rooms, elaborate mosaics and finely carved wood. At various places throughout the complex, raised slightly above the ground, are elongated slabs. These markers are the tombs of the Saadians, the dynasty that held power from the mid-16th to mid-17th century. Hidden and forgotten until the 1920s, their rediscovery unearthed one of the nicest sites in Marrakech, with cool gardens, fine artwork and a generally tranquil atmosphere.

ⓐ rue de Kasbah, Bab Agnaou ⓒ Daily 08.00–11.45, 14.00–17.45

Souks

Defined as Arabic or North African markets, Marrakech's souks are stalls and shops that sell a huge range of crafts, food and general goods. Located predominately to the north of the Jemaa, there are so many of these stalls running into each other that this entire area of the Medina seems to be one gigantic street market. Divided approximately according to the area of speciality, it's possible to navigate through this shopping maze based on the sorts of items visible. Narrow thoroughfares sell goods that relate to the main features on the larger routes, although some of these hideaways have their own sub-specialities. Usually under the cover of a slatted roof that lets in shafts of light, and so loaded with items that each stall seems to be overflowing, the souks can be somewhat claustrophobic, especially at peak times. Shopping at quieter periods might be easier, although the browser might be more subject to the full attention of the insistent salesman. Bargaining is the way to go, with virtually no stallholder giving his true lowest price at first request (see Bargaining, page 24).

A WALK IN THE MEDINA – SOUKS

Walking away from the Koutoubia across the Jemaa el Fna, turn left into any of the passageways crowded with goods. The souks begin here, and it's best to wander at will, the decision to turn left and right depending on what attracts the eye. At first overwhelming, it soon becomes apparent that the different souks specialise, and that it's possible to orient oneself depending on the type of item that's for sale.

Meandering more or less north, one comes eventually to the Place Ben Youssef, a less claustrophobic open square around which are located three of the Medina's major sights: the Ben Youssef Medersa, the Almoravid Qoubba and the Marrakech Museum. Head south again, choosing other passageways and different souks, to find your way back to the Jemaa.

Squares

Every so often, the cramped and crowded streets of the Medina give way to a spacious open space. Often, the square, or place, is worth attention in itself. Some of the more notable ones are:

Criée Berbère Emerging from the depths of the souk, here is where the carpet merchants show off their brightly coloured wares.

Ferblantiers In this very central location are the tinsmiths, producing all kinds of candleholders, lanterns and light fixtures.

Grand Mechouar This broad open space to the south of the Medina was attached to the Royal Palace, and once served as a waiting room.

Jemaa el Fna The most important square in Marrakech, see page 73.

Kissaria (also known as the Place Ben Youssef) More or less off this square are located three of Marrakech's most important sites, the Medersa Ben Youssef, the Almoravid Qoubba, and the Marrakech Museum.

Qzadria A pleasant park with benches and shade, this green space is a good place from which to navigate around the southern Medina.

Zaouias

Marrakech is an Islamic holy city, and still a pilgrimage destination, due to it being the final resting place of The Seven Saints. Living between the 12th and 16th centuries, the holies were: Sidi Cadi Ayad, Sidi As-Soheyli, Sidi Yousef Bin Ali, Sidi Bel Abbis, Sidi Bin Sliman Al Jazouli, Sidi Abdal Aziz Tebba and Sidi Al Ghazwani. The tomb of a marabout, or holy person, when it becomes the central focus of a mosque, is known as a *zaouia*. Although not open to non-Muslims, it's worth understanding the significance of these places when attempting a peak inside the mosque.

Some of the more important *zaouias* are **Sidi Abdel Aziz el Harrar** ❷ rue Mouassine; **Sidi Bel Abbes** ❷ rue Bab Taghzout; and **Sidi Ben Salah** ❷ place Ben Salah.

CULTURE

Most of the Medina's culture is visible on the streets, in its architecture, crafts and performances. There are very few formal museums.

Dar Bellarj

Once a hospital for injured storks, the *riad* was recently renovated and is now the Foundation for Moroccan Culture. Exhibitions on all aspects of national arts are held here. 9 rue Toualot Zaouiat Lakhdar ☎ 044 44 45 55 🕐 Daily 09.00–13.00, 14.00–18.30.

Dar Si Said

Located in a lavish palace, this assembly is also known as the South Morocco Regional Arts Museum. The collections include Berber jewellery, cedar-wood furniture, carpets, and window and door frames. ⓐ Riad Zitoun Jdid ☎ 044 38 95 64 🕐 Sat–Thur 09.00–11.45, 15.00–17.45, Fri 09.00–11.30, 15.00–17.45.

Dar Tiskiwin

Bert Flint, a Dutch art historian, exhibits his personal collection of traditional Moroccan art objects, within his own charming Hispano-Moorish style home. ⓐ 8 rue de la Bahia, Riad Zitoun Jdid ☎ 044 38 91 92 🕐 Daily 10.00–12.30, 15.00–18.30.

Ensemble Artisanal

Although primarily a series of shops, this complex is also an area of workshops for craftsmen. It's possible to watch artisans creating their specialist items *in situ*, without worrying about being hassled to buy. Prices are fixed and function as a good guide to how much items in the souks should cost.

ⓐ blvd Mohammed V ☎ 044 42 38 35 🕐 Daily 08.00–19.30.

Marrakech Museum

Previously a fabulous 19th-century palace, the building has now been converted to a large museum. Although changing exhibitions feature various aspects of traditional craft, the palace itself is what makes the visit worthwhile. ⓐ place Ben Youssef/ Kissaria ☎ 044 39 09 11 🕐 Daily 09.00–18.30.

NAMES OF THE SOUKS

The following is a list of some of Marrakech's souks, with the Arabic, and where they vary, French, names:

Arabic	French	English
Attarine		*brassware*
Cherratine	tanneurs	*tanners*
Chouari	ebenistes	*cabinet makers*
El Kebir	cuir	*leather*
Haddadine	fer	*iron*
Kassabine	épices	*spices*
Kchacha		*dried fruit, nuts, etc*
Kedima	apothecaries	*traditional medicine*
Kimakhine	des Musiciens	*instrument makers*
Laghzal	laine	*wool*
Sebbaghine	teinturier	*dyers*
Serrajine		*saddlers*
Smarine	textiles	*textiles*
Smata	babouches	*slippers*
Zarbia	tapis	*carpets*

RETAIL THERAPY

Shops & souks

Fruit, vegetable and fish markets spring up at will all over the Medina.

The main shopping area is just north of the Jemaa el Fna. Most shops are open daily, 09.00–18.00, and sometimes later in the souks. Lunch breaks, usually from 13.00–15.00, are not uncommon.

Al Yed Gallery Specialising in antique Berber jewellery, the shop also has an excellent collection of ceramics from the 12th to 19th centuries ❷ 66 Fhal Chidmi Mouassine ❶ 044 44 29 95.

Arts de Marrakech One among the many carpet stalls through Marrakech, you are certain of getting a good bargain here – if you negotiate hard enough! ❷ 85 place Rahba Kdima ❶ 044 44 53 85 ❺ Daily 08.00–20.00.

● *Souks are crammed with stalls that specialise in particular products*

Au Palais des Fossiles (The Palace of Fossils) Amonites and trilobites from the deserts of southern Morocco are for sale at this fun shop in the Kasbah. ❷ 37 place Moulay El Yazid, Kasbah ❶ 044 38 39 15.

Bab Music With the strains of Gnaoua music in the background, this subterranean storehouse features 1920s images of Marrakech, as well as musical instruments. ❷ 18 rue Goundafi, rue Riad Zitoun el Kdim ❶ 067 64 77 94 ❸ Daily 09.00–19.00.

Barradi Mohame ben Sadik Berber slippers in all colours dangle from the walls. It's also possible to find authentic 'Goodyear' examples, the soles made from real tyres. ❷ 38 souk Ahaik ❸ 09.00–20.00.

Beldi Hidden among the indistinguishable stalls in the souk, this little shop sells the finest – and most expensive – traditional Moroccan clothing. Prices are non-negotiable! ❷ 9–11 Souikat Laksour ❶ 044 44 10 76 ❸ Daily 09.00–13.00, 16.00–19.30.

Bellawi Abdellatif Antique clothing and Berber marriage belts are some of the things carried by this shop. More whimsical items like the pom-pom hats worn by the water sellers in the Jemaa are also on sale. ❷ rue Kissaria Lossta ❶ 044 44 01 07 ❸ Daily 09.00–19.30.

Centre artisanal et maison du tapis This large storehouse of Moroccan goods is adequate for shoppers who don't enjoy the intimacy (or claustrophobia) of the souk area but still want a wide selection of items. Located in the Kasbah district, far away from the rabble. ❷ 7 derb Baissi, rue de la Kasbah ❶ 044 38 18 53 ❸ Daily 09.00–19.00.

Chez Mustapha Lots of different varieties and colours of olives, as well as loads of different pickled fruit and vegetables, are on display here. ❷ 18 souk Ableuh ⏱ Daily 08.00–23.00.

Chez Redouane & Toufiq The artist/stallholder sells a range of goods, but the finest examples of his work are his handmade felt designer handbags. ❷ 1 Souk Labbadine, near the Souk des teinturiers ☎ 044 42 63 84.

Driss At the same location for over 35 years, this shop sells fine Jewish antiquities. ❷ 5 rue Mouassine ☎ 077 65 51 59.

El-Abidi Nasser Eddine This little store has exquisite Berber

CARPETS AND KILIMS

Whether in the Medina or travelling outside the city of Marrakech, it is hard to avoid these typical Moroccan craftwares. Both of these types of floor coverings are produced by traditional methods of weaving, although their forms are different.

A Moroccan carpet is a pile rug, which is knotted. The pile threads form the front and can be thick and heavy, with either a longer or shorter tuft. High Atlas rugs are quite soft with simple, graphic designs produced in a wide range of colours.

A kilim (or *hanbal*) is a rug that's flat woven, with the threads on the underside. Used more for hangings, covers and saddlebags, they are made by nomadic and semi-nomadic tribes often in very complex geometric patterns.

jewellery. Unlike most of the souks, prices here are fixed.
ⓐ 9 souk Smarine **ⓣ** 044 44 10 66 **ⓛ** Daily 09.00–20.30.

FNAC a branch of the large chain of stores that started in France, the stall sells books and batteries. In 1941, this corner shop was the first bookshop in Marrakech. **ⓐ** Souikat Laksour no. 64 **ⓣ** 044 44 34 17 **ⓛ** Daily 09.00–20.00.

Herboriste du Paradis Natural medicine and cosmetics are sold, as well as a bit of 'white magic'. **ⓐ** 93 place Ben Youssef **ⓣ** 044 42 72 49 **ⓛ** Daily 09.00–17.00.

Herboristerie Malih This spice market in the Mellah has an excellent selection of cooking herbs and spices. Alternative medicines are also for sale. **ⓐ** Hay Essalame, Mellah no. 184 **ⓣ** 044 38 74 03.

La Maison de caftan marocain (The House of the Moroccan caftan) A huge collection of fabulous Moroccan clothing of the highest quality is available here. This shop is also known for its famous clientele, with customers including Jean-Paul Gaultier and Alan Bates. **ⓐ** 65 rue Sidi-el-Yamani, Mouassine **ⓣ** 044 44 10 51 **ⓛ** Daily 08.00–20.00.

Le Monde de la Poupee (The World of the Doll) The artisan resident in the shop creates dolls made of fabric and dressed in traditional Moroccan style. Something a bit different from the usual souvenirs! **ⓐ** 114 Kissaria Hadj Abdeslam **ⓣ** 044 44 10 49. **ⓛ** Daily 09.00–19.00 (20.30 in summer).

La Qoubba Galerie A venue for displaying both new and established

Moroccan artists, this gallery is one of the better-known places to pick up some contemporary art. 🅰 91 Souk Talaa, place Ben Youssef/Kissaria 🕿 044 38 05 15 🕐 08.00–20.00.

No 18, Souk Stailia Ribbons, beads, buttons and embroidered borders are crammed into every available space in this little stall. 🕿 067 35 49 87.

No. 35, Souk Kimikhine Watch traditional musical instruments being produced at the back of the store, which is already full of wonderful examples.

No. 65, Souk Kimikhine War surplus, old posters, vintage Mickey Mouses and all sorts of oddments are packed into this tiny shop. A real treasure chest! 🅰 rue Sidi el Yamani, 65 rue Mouassine.

No 67, Souk Teinturier Original prints from photographers working in Marrakech in the 1920s are nicely displayed in the middle of the Dyers' market 🕿 060 44 96 32.

No. 132, Souk Teinturier Stone, marble and wood animals from all parts of the animal kingdom are for sale here. 🅰 by la fontaine Mouassine 🕐 Daily 09.00–19.00.

Original Design Wedged among the tinsmiths is this ceramics store, featuring finely made work in contemporary colours. 🅰 47 place des Ferblantiers 🕿 044 38 03 61 🕐 09.00–19.00.

◀ *Souks are just the place to find a useful souvenir of your visit*

Ouamhane Although all sorts of wooden items are found here, the shop specialises in games, such as backgammon and solitaire. ⓐ 27–29 souk el-Ghassoul ❶ 044 39 03 88 ❶ Daily 09.00–19.00.

Artisan Souffletier Unique gifts for friends who have fireplaces, or even for those who don't, these bellows are artisan-crafted and detailed in various different materials, including wood, leather and metal. ⓐ 10 Ensemble Artisanale, blvd Mohammed V ❶ Daily 08.00–13.00, 14.00–19.00.

Belkhou Mohamed Feutrier Wedged into a corner workshop within the Ensemble Artisanale, Belkou Mohamed first makes his felt by hand from goat's wool, then shapes it into some very attractive bags, carpets, hats and shoes. ⓐ 24 Ensemble Artisanale, blvd Mohammed V ❶ Daily 09.00–12.30, 14.00–19.00.

Benaddi Boujmaa All sorts of musical instruments, but especially traditional Moroccan ones, are built by this craftsman. Try your hand at playing some Gnaoua music! ⓐ Ensemble Artisanale, blvd Mohammed V ❶ 065 09 76 00 ❶ Daily 09.00–12.30, 14.00–19.00.

TAKING A BREAK

Bougainvillea Café A pleasant open courtyard in the middle of a renovated *riad* is the spot for this café-cum-art gallery. Good coffee, excellent cakes and savoury snacks are on offer. ⓐ 33 rue el Mouassine ❶ 044 44 11 11.

Café Argana Overlooking the Jemaa, the café on the third floor provides excellent views of activities in the square, as well as a good spot to take

a break. Good-value restaurants are on the floors underneath.
ⓐ 1–2 place Jemaa el Fna ⓣ 044 44 53 50 ⓛ Daily 05.00–23.00.

Café de France The outside tables provide excellent vantage points of the square, and the breakfasts are pretty good, too. This is one of the landmark cafés in the Medina, and as almost everyone knows where it is, a great meeting point. ⓐ place Jemaa el Fna ⓣ 044 44 13 19 ⓛ 05.00–23.00.

Café Jamal This casual café situated near the Kasbah is a great place to join the locals and watch football on television. ⓐ rue Jean du Pack, avenue Houmman ed Fetouaki ⓛ 06.00–21.00.

Café Palais el Badi On the upper terrace, this pleasant outdoor café is eye level with the storks of the Badi Palace. Stop for a light lunch or mint tea and look down at the action below. ⓐ 4 rue Touareg Berrima ⓣ 044 38 99 75 ⓛ 09.00–23.00.

Complexe Mabrouka Prominently placed on a major pedestrian street just off the Jemaa, the complex's café, ice cream parlour, patisserie and restaurant are right next to each other. Although there's nothing exotic on the menu, the food is decent French fare. ⓐ rue pietonnière Bab Agnaou ⓣ 044 44 24 26.

L'Etoile Just off the main square, this café is a great place to people-watch. ⓐ 55 rue Bab Agnaou ⓣ 044 44 19 52 ⓛ 06.00–24.00.

Marrakech Museum Café In the front courtyard of this museum is a delightful and low-key spot to wind down, and take a break. ⓐ place Ben Youssef / Kissaria ⓣ 044 38 99 75 ⓛ 09.00–18.00.

Patisserie-salon de thé des Princes A huge selection of both Moroccan and western pastries is available at this café, as well as ice cream. Sit inside, or take the goodies away. ⓐ 32 rue Bab Agnaou ⓣ 044 44 30 33 ⓛ Daily 05.00–21.00.

AFTER DARK

Chez Chegrouni D This cheap and cheerful café on the Jemaa is the landing point for the petit taxis that can get no further into the Medina. Watch the characters while getting basic tagines and couscous. ⓐ place Jemaa el Fna, rue des Banques ⓛ Daily, early till late.

Dar Mimouan D Good prices and ethnic cuisine are served in the courtyard of this old palace, even if the décor is a little over the top. ⓐ Riad Zitoun Kdim, Derb Ben Amrane 1 ⓣ 044 44 33 48 ⓛ Daily 09.00–23.00.

Jemaa el Fna D Eating at any of the stalls on the main square is an experience, and one way to select where to go is to see whose selection of food you like, as well as the number of locals huddled around the makeshift kitchens. No. 1 is good for couscous, no. 14 for fish, and no. 42 for an all-round mix. ⓐ place Jemaa el Fna ⓛ dusk till around 22.00.

Nid'cignognes D Literally beneath the storks, this simple low-key restaurant in the Kasbah is a good option for when the dirhams begin to run low. ⓐ 60 rue de la Kasbah ⓣ 044 38 20 92 ⓛ Daily 09.00–21.00

Le Toubkal D Another of the Jemaa's ringside cafés, this is a tourist favourite, offering local fare at basic prices. ⓐ place Jemaa el Fna, Riad Zitoun el Kdim ⓛ 06.00–24.00.

Dar Moha DD Known for its nouvelle cuisine versions of Moroccan standards, the ambience of this fine restaurant is enhanced by its poolside location. ⓐ 81 rue Dar el Bacha ⓣ 044 38 64 00 ⓛ Tues–Sun 12.00–15.00, 19.00–24.00.

Dar Timtam DD A salon-de-thé by day, and an eatery at night, this historic 19th-century palace now houses a fine restaurant. Hidden away behind a nondescript doorway, the courtyard is sumptuous. ⓐ rue Znikhet Rahba 044 39 14 46 ⓛ 09.00–21.00 but sometimes closed between lunch and dinner.

Fondouk DD Situated in the heart of the souks, this venue serves Moroccan cuisine but, unusually, blended with French Mediterranean flavouring – a nice change from the usual. ⓐ 55 Souk Hal Fassi Kat Bennahid ⓣ 044 37 81 90 ⓛ 12.00–24.00.

Jardins de la Medina DD One of Marrakech's finest *riads* serves some of its best food, in the courtyard of this delightful building. ⓐ 21 Derb Chtouka, Kasbah ⓣ 044 38 18 51 ⓦ www.lesjardinsdelamedina.com ⓛ 12.00–15.00, 19.00–22.30.

Le Marrakchi DD A fine restaurant that has one of the best views over the square and Koutoubia beyond, especially at sunset. This place is highly recommended for a first-night dinner. ⓐ rue des Banques, place Jemma el Fna ⓣ 044 44 33 77 ⓛ Daily 12.00–15.00, 19.00–22.30 ⓦ www.lemarrakchi.com

Narwama DD Overshadowed by the high-profile Jardins de la Koutoubia hotel, this predominantly Thai restaurant occupies a huge courtyard in one of the Medina's surprisingly large hidden locations. Makes a nice change from couscous! 30 rue Koutoubia 044 44 08 44.

Les Terraces de Alhambra DD Straddled over three storeys, these terraces serve breakfast, lunch and dinner while overseeing the changing activities of the Jemaa below. As well as the usual standards there are also pastas on the menu. place Jemaa el Fna, face au Café de France 044 42 75 70 07.00–24.00.

La Rotonda DDD A restaurant legendary for its excellent Italian-Moroccan food, the cooking is variable and prices are a bit steep. Still, on a good day, eating here can be a superb experience. 39 Derb Lamnabha, rue de la Kasbah 044 38 15 85.

Le Pavillon DDD In this tastefully decorated *riad* lies, quite possibly, the best French restaurant in the city. Indulge in gastronomic standards with Moroccan accents, such as foie gras and bouillabaisse. Derb Zaouia, Bab Doukkala 044 38 70 40 Wed–Mon, dinner only.

Le Yacout DDD Marrakech's most exclusive restaurant is where the glitterati go when they want to be seen. The best of the best Moroccan food is served in this gorgeous 17th-century Arab residence. 79 rue Sidi Ahmed Soussi 044 38 29 29.

Bars

Churchill Piano Bar Dark and inviting, and clearly paying homage to the Mamounia's most famous British guest, this bar in the depths of the hotel offers alcohol – at a price! Hotel Mamounia, Avenue Bab Jdid, Medina 044 38 86 00 www.mamounia.com

Grand Hotel Tazi A little grubby, and right in the middle of things, this bar is one of the few places where you can get a beer in the old town. A well-known backpackers' hotel and hang-out, the cheap prices are very much appreciated by the clientele. ❸ Angle Av. El Mouahidine et Rue Bab Agnaou, Medina ❶ 044 44 27 87.

Piano Bar, Jardins de la Koutoubia Very upmarket, this comfortable place is located within a luxury hotel. It's a perfect spot for having a drink after watching the activities at the nearby Jemaa el Fna. ❸ 26 rue de la Koutoubia ❶ 44 38 88 00 ❼ www.lesjardinsdelakoutoubia.com/anglais

Casino
Le Grand Casino de la Mamounia Technically just within the city walls, the Mamounia has a casino where you can bet away whatever cash you may have. Like the rest of the facilities at the hotel, the gambling area is very upmarket, and a dress code applies. ❸ Avenue Bab Jdid, Medina ❶ 044 38 86 00 ❼ www.mamounia.com ❶ Daily, machines from 16.00, main gaming hall from 20.00.

Cinemas
Cinema Eden Marrakech's oldest cinema invites locals and tourists alike to cram together in this little space, filled with folding chairs. The latest films are shown here, but they're just as likely to be Kung Fu movies as Hollywood blockbusters. ❸ rue Riad Zitoun Jdid, rue des Banquets.

Cinema Mabrouka This very popular venue right in the heart of the Medina's main pedestrian street shows Bollywood, Hollywood and martial arts movies. ❸ rue Pietonnière, Bab Agnaou ❶ 044 44 24 26.

Guéliz (Ville Nouveau) & the Palmeraie

Soon after the Treaty of Fes was signed in 1912, which changed Morocco's status from an independent country to a colony of France, a town planner arrived to develop a new city in Marrakech alongside the old. The French section was deliberately arranged in an organised fashion, a complete contrast to the organic convolutions of the Medina, with a line to the north-west, now the main boulevard Mohammed V, and one to the south-west, now avenue de la Menara. Named after the Catholic church, *iglise*, of Saint Anne, the name degraded into Guéliz.

The modern town is nowhere near as fascinating as the Medina, but it does hold a few things of interest for the tourist. The Majorelle Gardens are the area's prime attractions, while upmarket shopping can certainly be found in the district. Far more bars, clubs and discos operate here, as the stringent Islamic anti-alcohol laws are not as potent as in the old town.

The Palmeraie, about 20 km (12 miles) to the northeast of Marrakech, is the city's newest fashionable area. Once an enclave of palms, the trees have been literally falling to make way for houses for the rich and famous, luxury hotels, golf courses and stables. There are no historic attractions here, other than a few camels hanging around the remains of the original oasis waiting for riders, but the resort facilities are excellent.

SIGHTS & ATTRACTIONS

Abd El Moumen Ben Ali Square

The heart of Guéliz, this square is not an attraction in its own right, but rather more important as the effective centre of the new city.

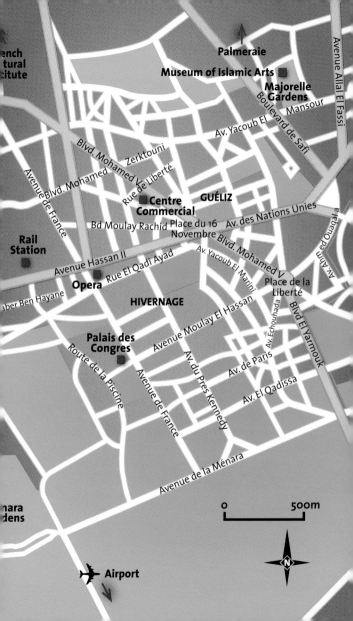

Always busy, at the junction of the main Mohammed V and Mohammed Zerktouni boulevards, the area is noisy and full of life at any time of the day.

Boulevard Mohammed V

Marrakech's main thoroughfare stretches from the north-western corner of the Medina through Guéliz, passing some of the city's most important buildings along the way. It's worthwhile remembering this street for orientation.

Centre Commercial

Just off the main boulevard is the Centre Commercial. Located within an office block and mostly full of souvenirs, this collection of shops is nowhere near as comprehensive as the souks of the Medina. Nevertheless, if time is pressing, and opportunity doesn't allow for meandering, most tourist goods can be purchased here. ❷ Ibn Toumert.

Majorelle Gardens

This magnificent collection of exotic plants, gathered around the bright blue former residence of its original owner, the artist Jacques Majorelle, is a wonderful respite in the new town. After Majorelle's death, the gardens started disintegrating and there was talk of using the grounds for urban development. In 1962, the fashion designer Yves Saint-Laurent and his partner, the artist Pierre Bergé, bought the park and brought it up to its current glorious condition. It's a pleasure to wander through this lush greenery made more striking by the occasional pot or detail in a bright, contrasting

---

▶ *The peace of the Majorelle gardens contrast with life in the Medina*

colour. The Museum of Islamic Arts now resides inside the main azure building. ⓐ Yacoub el Mansour ⓘ 044 30 18 52 ⓛ Daily 08.00–18.30.

Menara Gardens

At the far western end of the city are these 250 acres of gardens, filled with olive groves. Open to the public, people come here, especially on Fridays and Sundays, to stroll around the grounds and picnic. In the centre is a reservoir, in existence since the 12th century, which the Almohads built to supply water to the Medina. The pavilion, constructed in the 19th century by the sultan Moulay Abd

er Rahman, is a pleasing visual focus, especially in the winter, when the reflections of the snow-covered High Atlas Mountains are visible in the lake. ⓐ avenue de la Menara ⓒ Daily 05.00–18.30.

Opera/Theatre Royal

In the Hivernage section of the new town, this impressive multi-functional arts complex is an striking landmark near the railway station. Built in a Moroccan-classical style, with its row of palm trees alongside, the newly completed main building dominates the urban

⬥ Marrakech's newest attraction is the home of its opera and theatre

landscape. The auditorium is home to the Royal Theatre, as well as the venue for visiting performing arts groups and the occasional conference. ⓐ avenue de France ⓣ 044 43 15 16 ⓛ 08.00–12.00, 14.00–18.30, closed public holidays.

Palais des Congrès

Typical of the new modern Moroccan architecture, this massive building is used for international meetings, as well as for conferences. In 1994, the Palais was the place where the GATT agreements were signed, establishing the World Trade Organization. ⓐ avenue de France ⓣ 044 33 91 00.

PALMERAIE

Among the posh housing estates and flashy new hotels in the area remains the last of the original Palmeraie, or palm grove. Suffering diseases, not to mention urban development, the vestiges of the original 100,000 trees are still hanging in there.

Take a late-afternoon *calèche* along the circuit, especially just before dusk, to catch a glimpse of the ancient date palm groves in the desert. Alternatively, if you want the experience and can handle the sway, hop on the back of one of the camels waiting to show tourists around.

ⓐ 20 km (12 miles) north-east of Marrakech, route de Fes and route de Casablanca.

Place du 16 Novembre

This centrally located square with its fountain is another good orientation point, even if the architecture to the north is block ugly. To the south-west is the Harti garden, simple and pleasant, with its alley of olive trees and a small playground for children.

● *The distinctive home of the Museum of Islamic Art*

Rue de la Liberté

In the heart of Guéliz, this small street has a disproportionate number of fine shops. Ranging from gourmet pastries to elegant interior decoration, this avenue is a complete contrast to the souk experience, with no bartering allowed!

CULTURE

French Cultural Institute

This venue has a varying programme of cultural events, including dance, film and theatre events. The organisation features prominently during the International Film Festival. ❸ route de Targa ❶ 044 44 69 30 ❿ www.ambafrance-ma.org

Galerie Bleu

Here is a gallery that displays the work of more interesting contemporary Moroccan artists, particularly those whose vision is a bit different from the usual. Items are for sale, but prices are high enough that the venue functions more as a display arena than a shop. ❸ 119 blvd Mohammed V ❶ 044 42 00 80 ❸ Tues–Sun 10.00–13.00, 16.00–20.00.

Museum of Islamic Arts in the Majorelle Gardens

Once the home of the gardens' eponymous artist-owner, the gorgeous blue house in the middle of the plants has been converted to the showplace of Pierre Berge and Yves Saint-Laurent's art collection. Now called the Museum of Islamic Arts, the assembly features distinctive Moroccan pieces from all over the country. ❸ Majorelle Gardens, Yacoub el Mansour ❶ 044 30 18 52 ❸ Daily 08.00–12.00, 14.00–18.30.

RETAIL THERAPY

Intensité Nomade Quite possibly the trendiest in Marrakech and certainly one of the more expensive, this boutique sells Moroccan-influenced fashion made from the finest natural materials. Clothing for both men and women in stock. ❸ 139 blvd Mohammed V ❶ 044 43 13 33 ❸ Mon–Sat 09.00–12.30, 15.00–20.00.

Librairie ACR Find the art publication you've been looking for at this specialist bookshop. Pick up a book on cooking or design while

❹ *The Centre Commercial is a good place to find souvenirs in Guéliz*

you're here, and maybe even a postcard or two! blvd Mohammed Zerktouni, residence Tayeb 044 44 67 92 Mon–Sat 09.00–12.30, 15.00–19.30.

L'Orientaliste A charming mixed bag of a place, with old bottles, copper bowls, candlesticks, early 20th-century engravings, Fes pottery and all sorts of antiques. 15 rue de la Liberté 044 43 40 74 Mon–Sat 09.00–12.30, 15.00–19.30, Sun 09.00–13.00.

Mamounia Arts A branch of the famous hotel's art gallery is located in the heart of Guéliz. Fine collectables are on display, including jewellery, arms and 'old curiosities'. 7 rue de la Liberté 044 42 02 00 Daily 08.00–20.00.

Place Vendome Beautiful leather and fine fashion items are for sale in this well-known shop. Though not as cheap as in the souks, the quality is indisputable. 141 avenue Mohammed V 044 43 52 63 Mon–Sat 09.00–12.30, 15.00–19.30, Sun 09.00–13.00.

Scènes de Lin An interior decorator's paradise, Anne-Marie Chaoui shows her beautiful products, including fabrics and furniture, to a more discerning, and wealthier, clientele. 70 rue de la Liberté 044 43 61 08 Mon–Sat 09.00–12.30, 15.00–19.30.

Unitex Clothing for children is this store's speciality, ideal for younger fashion-conscious clients, although all members of the family can find something to wear here. 35–36 ave Moulay-el-Hassan, Centre Kawkab 044 43 04 65 Mon–Sat 09.00–12.30, 15.00–20.00. Hours may vary in summer.

TAKING A BREAK

Amandine Grab a mouth-watering pastry to take away from the well-stocked patisserie, or sit down and enjoy a coffee or snack at the space next door. ⓐ 177 rue Mohammed el Behal ⓣ 044 44 96 12 ⓛ Daily 06.00–23.00.

Boule de Neige The usual range of patisserie and drinks, both cold and hot, is available, but the highest recommendation goes to the air conditioning, particularly in the summer. ⓐ 30 rue de Yougoslavie ⓣ 044 44 60 44 ⓛ Daily 05.00–23.00.

Café les Negociants Watch the activity at the buzzing Abd El Moumen Ben Ali Square while sipping a coffee or mint tea at this sidewalk café. ⓐ Abd El Moumen Ben Ali Square, avenue Mohammed V ⓣ 044 43 57 82 ⓛ Daily 06.00–23.00.

Glacier Oliveri The ice cream is famous, but the pastries here are also delicious. Come for breakfast, too. ⓐ 7–9 bld E-Mansour Eddahbi ⓣ 044 44 89 13 ⓛ Daily 06.00–23.00.

La Marjolaine This French-style café serves snacks and pizzas as well as ice cream and coffee. Slightly more elegant than the usual pizza parlours, it's well located on the main drag. ⓐ 234 immeduble Zahir, avenue Mohammed V.

Michéle Bacconier Among the clothing and souvenirs lurks this rather smart tea house, where salads are also served. Not the cheapest, but nice nevertheless. ⓐ 6 rue du Vieux Marrakchi ⓣ 044 44 91 78 ⓛ Mon–Sat 09.00–19.30, Sun 09.00– 12.30.

Patisserie chez Mirgon Celebrated for both its French and Moroccan pastry, come here for a dessert for your picnic. ⓐ 151 avenue Mohammed V ⓣ 044 43 01 94 ⓛ Daily 07.00–12.30, 16.00–20.00.

Venezia Ice This ice cream stand sits at the base of the Hotel Islane, just across from the Koutoubia. The flavours are creative and

Café les Negociants is a great place for people-watching

delicious, and the scoops very reasonably priced. ⓐ 2790 av Mohammed V ⓣ 044 42 96 04.

AFTER DARK

Restaurants

Rotisserie de la Paix D As the name says, the speciality of this outdoor venue is various types of meat grilled over a wood fire. In the shade at lunchtime, or under the lights in the evening, sitting in the garden is always pleasant. ⓐ 68 rue de Yougoslavie ⓣ 044 43 31 18 ⓛ Daily 12.00–15.00, 19.00–23.00.

Sindibad D Open 24 hours a day, a rarity for Marrakech, decent basic tagines, couscous and other Moroccan staples are served at all hours. ⓐ 3 blvd Mohammed V ⓣ 044 43 01 36.

Al Fassia DD The outstanding feature is the food (rather than the décor), as the woman who runs the restaurant brings her own classic Fes-style cooking to the table. Consistently good, and always busy, it's essential to book ahead. ⓐ 232 blvd Mohammed V ⓣ 044 43 40 60 ⓛ Daily 12.00–14.30, 20.00–24.00.

Bagatelle DD The French dining experience is authentic enough to provide wine and beer with meals. Gallic cuisine is served in the outdoor vine-covered terrace, or in the dining room. ⓐ 101 rue de Yougoslavie ⓣ 044 43 02 74 ⓛ Thur–Tues 12.00–15.00, 19.00–23.00.

La Trattoria DD Some of the best Italian dishes in the city are augmented by the Hispano-Moorish 1920s-style decor. Outdoor tables flank the pool, while the rooms in which the indoor ones sit

are legendary ⓐ 179 rue Mohammed El Bekal ⓣ 044 43 26 41
ⓦ www.latrattoriamarrakech.com ⓛ Daily 19.00–23.30.

Pizza Venezia DD The Hotel Islane's top terrace doubles as an Italian restaurant, with a large variety of pastas as well as a good selection of pizzas. The views of the Koutoubia, especially in the evening, are lovely. ⓐ Hotel Islane, 279 blvd Mohammed V ⓣ 044 44 00 81.

Bars, clubs & discos

Le Diamont Noir With a less expensive entrance charge than the fashionable clubs, this hang-out attracts a varied crowd, more interested in having a good time than with looks. There's also an active gay scene here. ⓐ Hotel Le Marrakech, place de la Liberté ⓣ 044 43 43 51 ⓛ Daily 22.00–dawn.

Le New Feeling Way out in the Palmeraie is this trendy club, once the haunt of the present king. The local partying residents are often the film stars and personalities who have their houses nearby. ⓐ Palmeraie Golf Palace ⓣ 044 30 10 10 ⓛ Daily 22.00–dawn.

Le Theatro Just next to the Hotel Saadi's casino, the club's DJ plays an eclectic range of music, ranging from techno and house to Moroccan and R'n'B. ⓐ Avenue El Quadissia, Hivernage ⓣ 044 44 88 11.

Montecristo Salsa and samba dominate the upstairs dance floor, while the rooftop is the place to sip cocktails or down a beer. Nibble on some tapas, or take a puff on a cigar, both for sale here. ⓐ 20 rue ben Aicha ⓣ 044 43 90 31 ⓛ Daily 19.00–02.00.

ⓞ *Shopping in the newer part of the city is considered slightly more upmarket*

Paradise Within the Hotel Kempinski is this disco/club whose clientele seems to be mostly affluent Moroccans. Music blares and lights flash over the packed dance floor. ⓐ Kempinski Mansour, avenue de France, Hivernage ⓣ 044 33 91 00 ⓛ Daily 23.00 till dawn.

Cinemas

La Colisée Possibly the best cinema in Marrakech, it's certainly comfortable, and one of the more popular local venues. ⓐ blvd Mohammed Zerktouni ⓣ 044 44 88 93.

Rif This 800-seat movie house plays the usual range of films suited to the Moroccan taste, taken from both the Asian and western traditions. ⓐ Cite Mohammadia (near the Palmeraie) ⓣ 044 30 31 46.

Events & shows

Al Menara Using the latest sound and light technology, this show combines visual effects with live performers to produce a magnificent outdoor show at the Menara Gardens. Reflections in the large pool double the effect. ⓐ Menara Gardens ⓣ 044 43 95 80 ⓛ Wed–Mon 21.00 (closed January, February).

Chez Ali Ostensibly a tourist version of the Festival of Popular Arts, the dinner combo takes elements from Moroccan culture and th *One Thousand and One Nights* tales and puts on a show of dance, music and folklore. The horsemanship is pretty amazing. ⓐ Circuit de la Palmeraie ⓣ 044 30 77 30 ⓦ www.ilove-marrakesh.com/chezali

---

ⓞ *Sunset is the time for a camel ride on the beach at Essaouira*

OUT OF TOWN
trips

The High Atlas Mountains

Even on summer days it's impossible not to be aware of the impressive backdrop to the city of Marrakech, and on winter ones the snow-covered High Atlas Mountains are extremely impressive. The alpine-like environment is as close as it looks, and it's less than 100 km (about 60 miles) away from the city to the base of North Africa's tallest mountain, at 4165 m (13,665 ft). In fact, within minutes of passing through Marrakech's border ramparts to the south the landscapes changes to rural Morocco. Soon, the contours begin, as well as the agricultural terraces and villages that seem to be carved out of the hills themselves. The roads get narrower, the scenery and views increasingly dramatic as the road passes small towns, and, if on the right day, the regional markets. Within a couple of hours, the landscape becomes rugged and truly mountainous, whether in the warm haze of summer or the chilly frost of winter.

Four main routes lead to the Atlas, two of which continue to destinations on the other side of the range, and two that go no further. The most easterly is the Tizi n'Tichka road, a dramatic and fairly safe highway that leads to the city of Ouarzazate, 225 km (140 miles) away, and points further south. The furthest west is the drive that goes as far south as Amizmiz, about 55 km (34 miles) from Marrakech, passing the village of Tamesloht and its interesting Kasbah, as well as the Lalla Takerkoust Dam and reservoir. The middle two thoroughfares are the ones that are the most worthwhile for short trips: The Tizi n' Test is a difficult but interesting road that leads to Taroudant, 3.5 hours way, but before it gets tricky, branches off to Imlil and the beginning of the Mount Toubkal ascent. Another short trip option is to the Ourika Valley and the town of Setti Fatma, about 62 km (39 miles), although the ski

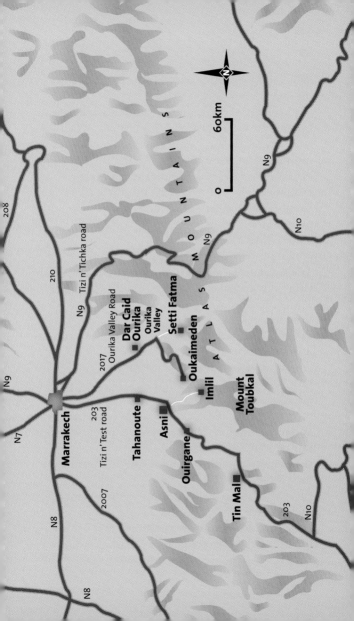

resort of Oukaimeden is accessible beforehand via a turn-off along this road.

It's possible to get to most of the major destinations via bus, leaving from the main station near Bab Doukkala in Marrakech. However, when travelling by public transport, you are subject to local timetables that can be inconvenient. A better option is to hire a Grand Taxi (Petit Taxis are not allowed beyond the city limits), negotiating fares and rendezvous points with the drivers. The easiest, though certainly not the cheapest, option is to hire a car.

SIGHTS & ATTRACTIONS

To Imlil and Tin Mal, via the Tizi n'Test Road (203 to Taroudant)
Distances given are from Marrakech.

Tahanoute (32 km/20 miles)
Lying at 1000 m (3300 ft) above sea level, with the Reghaia river below, this little village comes to life on Tuesdays and Saturdays, when it stages its enormous rural market.

Moulay Ibrahim
Just past Tahanoute on a side road is a little enclave famous for its eponymous shrine, and the pilgrims who come from all around to see it. A moussem, or organised pilgrimage, takes place every year. Of more interest to non-Muslims are the gorges that are just to the north of the hamlet.

Asni (45 km/28 miles)
The largest town en route is famous for its Saturday market. Full of local produce, livestock and Moroccan 'food halls', the bazaar

provides a fascinating insight into rural life. Look out for the donkey, aka Berber Mercedes, 'parking lot'. Asni itself is pleasant enough and offers great views of the towering peaks surrounding the place.

Imlil (62 km/39 miles)
Turning left at the fork from Asni, and following it to the end of the paved road, one comes to this thriving little town in the heart of the High Atlas foothills. Serving as a centre for all the Berber villages that lie along the crests and high up in the mountains, Imlil is a microcosm of a big town, with most goods and facilities that locals

The market comes to the mountains at Tahanoute

might want, albeit on a miniature scale. Even primary schools are provided (the closest secondary is in Asni). Imlil and the nearby Kasbah du Toubkal are excellent bases for hikes into the peaks, including the ascent of Mount Toubkal. Guides and provisions can be acquired here.

Kasbah du Toubkal

The owners have renovated this hilltop citadel and done a magnificent job. Framed against the background of North Africa's highest peaks, the massive construction serves as a hotel, restaurant, hammam and hiking centre. Single and multi-day trips with Berber guides can be organised from Marrakech with a brief – or longer – stopover here.

Ouirgane (60 km/37 miles)

This little village amongst the pine trees, on the main Tizi n' Test road, is known as an excellent starting point for Atlas treks, as well as for delightful guesthouses. It's a good place from which to hike or horseback ride, where it's still possible to spend the night in comfort.

Tin Mal (100 km/62 miles)

The 12th-century Almohad dynasty began life here, revering this little town as its holy city. Sections of the original medieval ramparts are still visible. They are, however, overshadowed by the recently restored mosque that non-Muslims are allowed to visit.

To Setti Fatma and Oukaimeden via the Ourika Valley Road (2017)

Aghmat (28 km/17 miles)

Reached by a 2 km (1.5 mile) dirt track off the main road, are the

SKIING IN AFRICA

One of the most exotic, not to mention unusual, places in the world for winter sports is at Oukaimeden, just outside Marrakech. At an altitude of 3258 m (10,689 ft), with a vertical drop of 663 m (2175 ft) and 20 pistes measuring 20 km (12 miles) in total, this French-developed resort can be a great place to ski when the snowfall is decent.

Donkeys supply a uniquely Moroccan touch, providing transport to runs that the lifts don't service. Passes and ski equipment rental are very reasonably priced. In good years, the resort can get pretty crowded on weekends, when the Marrakchi take advantage of their proximity and get in all the skiing they can.

remains of an ancient Almoravid city. The grave of the 11th-century poet king El Moutamid rests in the town, together with his shrine.

Dar Caid Ourika (40 km/25 miles)
This town comes into its own in Mondays, when it stages a weekly market for the inhabitants of this area.

Setti Fatma (62 km/38 miles)
At the end of the Ourika Valley, as well as the road, is this village known for its saint, and the moussem held in his honour every year in August. More of a fair than a religious event, it attracts families as well as the occasional mystic. For the rest of the year, the place is better known for its seven cascades, a hike for which a guide is recommended and certainly available.

Oukaimeden (77 km/48 miles)

Morocco's main ski resort lies at the heart of the High Atlas Range, at an altitude of 2600 m (8530 ft). Between December and March enough snow usually falls to cover the entire region and allow the chairlifts, rope tows and equipment rental to operate. Accommodation is available in various styles, ranging from a four-star luxury hotel to a mountain refuge. In the summer, the area is much less visited, although quite a few hikes begin from here.

RETAIL THERAPY

> **MARKET DAYS**
>
> Much of the region's buying activity is done through the weekly markets. Although not really for tourists, the bazaars are extremely interesting, especially for experiencing a bit of local life. The days for some of the larger town's gatherings are:
>
> **Aghmat** Friday
> **Asni** Saturday
> **Dar Caid Ourika** Monday
> **Ouirgane** Thursday
> **Setti Fatma** Thursday
> **Tahanoute** Tuesday

Alongside the roads are several small shops selling ammonites, trilobites and 'minerals' that come from the deserts of south Morocco. The fossils are usually real, although a certain amount of

● *Oukaimeden is the country's main ski resort*

perusing can determine if they're fake. The 'minerals' are very often rocks that have been artificially coloured or enhanced. Be very wary regarding their authenticity, and unless you are sure they're genuine or simply like the look of them, don't buy them.

Carpet sellers peddle their wares all over Morocco, and the road to the Atlas is one of their strongholds. The floor mats are usually legitimate, and often quite beautiful, but the sales patter can be a bit overwhelming. However, if you're sincerely interested in purchasing rugs, the mountains can be a good location to acquire them. It's best to do some research in Marrakech to discover the going rate, before practising bargaining in the highlands.

Amazouz Mohamed One among many little shops on the main street of Imlil's village, this place has a good selection of Berber craft articles, including fabrics and slippers. Starting prices are very reasonable. ② Douar Armed, Imlil ① 062 49 47 01.

Brahim Air Mbark Sales staff are honest about their wares, which include fossils and Berber silver jewellery. They are fairly knowledgeable about their products' authenticity and manufacture and prices are very negotiable. ② Dour Aremd, Imlil ① 070 60 15 87.

La source du tapis Perhaps a little more expensive, but also more reliable, this carpet and kilim shop exports all over the world. ② BP 18, Vallée Amassir, Ourika ① 044 48 44 58.

TAKING A BREAK

Most of the roadside shops and many of the towns have tiny cafés or, at the very least, places where mint tea is served. Negotiations for goods frequently include a small tea ceremony as part of the process. All the markets serve fresh squeezed orange juice and often pastry, such as doughnuts.

Au Sanglier Qui Fume This basic lodge is located on the Tizi n'Test road, about 60 km (37 miles) south of Marrakech. With pleasant surroundings and a covered terrace, it's a nice place to stop for lunch. Accommodation and dinner are also available. ❷ on the left in the village of Ouirgane ❶ 044 48 57 07.

Café Soleil This café is where visitors and locals hang out in Imlil, usually on the outdoor terrace. Reasonably priced rooms are another of the services offered. ❸ Centre Imlil ❶ 044 48 56 22.

Tichka Atlas With views of the valley below, and the Berber villages above, this restaurant is well located for a break between the morning and afternoon hikes. ❷ BP 29 (400 m/437 yds from the centre of Imlil) route de Tachedirte ❶ 044 48 52 23.

ACCOMMODATION

Auberge le Maquis D Clean, colourful and with lovely views, this former hunting lodge is a nice base for hiking in the Ourika Valley. The price includes dinner or lunch ❸ Km 45, Aghbalou Ourika par Marrakech ❶ 044 48 45 31 ❾ www.le-maquis.com

Chez Juju D A reasonable place to stay for a ski break, the price for an overnight stay at this very good hotel, in the centre of Oukaimeden, includes full board. Skis, poles and boots are available for hire in the nearby shops. ❷ BP 695 Station de Ski, Oukaimeden ❶ 044 45 90 05.

Chez Momo D Experience a real Berber ambience in this charming little rural inn, nestling at the base of the Atlas and serving authentic regional cuisine. Momo was born in the village and reveres the tradition of hospitality. 🅐 Km 61, Centre Ouirgane, CP 42 150 Par Marrakech 🅣 044 48 57 04 🅦 www.aubergemomo.com

Club Alpin Français D This organisation runs several refuges in the area, in association with the Youth Hostel Association. Used mostly for overnight stays for trekkers, the accommodation consists primarily of multi-bedded dorm rooms.
Chalet: Oukaimeden. Refuges: du Imlil, Tachedirte, Tazaghart, Toubkal.
🅣 0 44 31 90 36 🅦 www.cafmaroc.co.ma/chaletlouka/chalet.asp

Hotel Etoile du Toubkal D Cheap and cheerful, this basic hotel is located right in the heart of the village. A few rooms have baths 🅐 BP 105, Imlil 🅣 044 48 56 13.

Kasbah du Toubkal DD This beautifully renovated Kasbah sits on up a hill (hike or mule ride required) at the base of Mount Toubkal. Room options range from shared dorms to entire apartments. The Kasbah also offers lunch and dinner, and guided tours to the neighbouring villages, as well as treks into the mountains. Winner of a Green Globe Award for Sustainable Tourism.
🅐 Imlil. For information, contact Discover Ltd, Timbers, Oxted Road, Godstone, Surrey RH9 8AD, UK 🅣 44 (0) 1883 744392
🅦 www.kasbahdutoubkal.com

Kenzi Louka DD At an altitude of 2600 m (8530 ft), this four-star hotel in the Oukaimeden ski area looks just like an upmarket French resort, with all its facilities. It's open all year, although its high season is the winter. ❷ Oukaimeden ❶ 044 31 90 80 ❿ www.kenzi-hotels.com/anglais/hotels/ouka/ouka.html

Residence La Roseraie DDD This fabulous residence is an exercise in luxury. With a spa, three pools, private terraces, excellent food and horse riding, staying here is truly an indulgence. Save up your dirhams and spend a few delicious days here. ❷ Ouirgane ❶ 044 43 91 28.

⊙ *Kasbah du Toubkal offers elegant accommodation, and meals*

Essaouira

Charming, cooled by constant ocean breezes, and with a relaxed atmosphere, this seaside town still has enough going on to make it a happening place. Much smaller and certainly lower-key than Marrakech, Essaouira's distinctive colours and lovely location attract both foreign and domestic artists and tourists. Buildings painted blue and white are complemented by the occasional splash of yellow. Craftsmen sell their wares in the Medina and underneath the town walls, while painters exhibit their work both in galleries and the Medina's streets. Located on a rocky outcrop extending into the Atlantic Ocean, one of the town's outstanding features is its 18th-century rampart that not only protects the city's heart but also functions as a maritime battlement. Fortified to prevent successful attacks from the sea, the row of cannons that peaks out through gaps in the barriers is one of the more interesting legacies.

Essaouira's location has made it a viable port since Phoenician times. Visited by representatives from most of the ancient Mediterranean powers, Romans set up a trading post during the 1st century BC. A factory was established when the inhabitants discovered that the local purpura shells could be ground up and made into a royal purple colour. Called Amogdoul after an 11th-century saint, Sidi Mogdoul, who was buried there, the early 16th-century Portuguese invaders renamed it Mogador. By the mid-century, the Moroccans claimed back the city, and two hundred years later, in 1776, the sultan used the skills of a French engineer, captured during a failed invasion, to redesign the city. For a while the town was known as Saouira, 'the small fortress', but gradually changed to 'Es-Saouira', 'the beautifully designed', after its transformation. In its heyday, the port was the main outlet for the

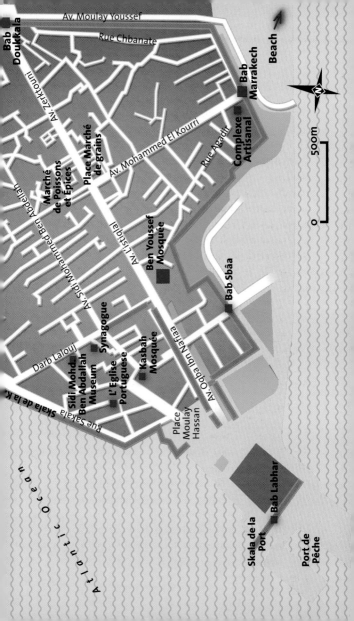

Timbuktu caravans. The development of the larger Agadir drew trade away from Essaouira and slowly the smaller town was reduced to being merely a fishing port. Tourism, however, began and has now evolved into a major economic force.

In the 1950s, the director and actor Orson Welles succumbed to Essaouira's appeal and used its walls in his film *Othello*. In the 1960s, the city was discovered as part of the Hippy Trail, and its most famous visitor from this era was Jimi Hendrix (as placards in various places within the Medina will not let 21st-century tourists forget!). Although still retaining its charm, development is continuing, mostly outside the Medina. The ocean provides some of the best windsurfing in North Africa, and hotels and resorts are

⬇ *This seaside resort is also a working fishing port*

being constructed to cater to this new source of revenue. For those less willing to brave the cold Atlantic waters, beachside horse and camel riding are available a brief stroll away from the city centre.

SIGHTS & ATTRACTIONS

Babs

The Medina, or ancient centre, is protected by a complete wall with various entry points, or Babs, providing access to the heart. Some of these openings are very dramatic, including:

Bab Doukkala The northern-most gate date back to the city's 18th-century facelift and was designed to be the principal entrance to the city.

Bab Labhar Also known as the Porte de la Marine, this impressive arch is the gateway to the fishing harbour from the Medina.

Bab Marrakech The only breach in the wall built for defence against attacks from the east, various artists and artisans now reside and display in this area.

Bab Sbâa Leading directly to blvd Mohammed V, the main highway from both Marrakech and Agadir, this portal is the one that most visitors see first.

Beach

The beautiful west-facing strand extends for miles. Protected by islands in the bay, the sea is normally relatively flat and it's a pleasure to wade through the gentle surf. Together with the constant breezes, the town has developed an excellent reputation for windsurfing, with facilities and rentals widely available. Some beachside hotels cater especially for the sport. Further along the bay, horses and camels wait for tourists to enjoy the stroll on four legs (try Argaibi Mohammed, ☎ 070 57 79 41).

Iles Purpuraies

A series of little islands out to the west of the bay provides not only cover for the beach, but also a lovely backdrop, especially as the sun goes down.

Now designated as an area of special scientific interest, landing visits are not allowed, although it is possible to sail in the area. Vestiges of ancient habitation remain, including ruins of the purpure (purple) factories, and a Portuguese fort on the Island of Mogador.

Place Prince Moulay El Hassan

At the southern end of the Medina is a main square that leads down to the port. The largest open space within the old city, here is where many outdoor cafés and restaurants reside. Always buzzing, this spot is ideal for morning breakfast, mid-morning coffee, light lunch, afternoon mint tea, or even a bit of sunset watching.

Port de peche

Dramatically guarded by the centuries-old Porte de la Marine, the fishing port is a fascinating place. When the boats come in, the activity is raucous, fishermen unloading their often exotic catch, seagulls squawking in hope and both tourists and locals standing around to watch. At other times, nets are strewn about with men rapidly unwinding or repairing them. Most interesting, however, is the traditional boat-building and repair. Up on plinths, the vessels in various sizes and colours, and all states of assembly and renovation, dominate the skyline of the harbour.

Religious buildings

Some of the different faiths that serviced Essaouira in the past are still represented by their prayer houses. The city today has 18 mosques, 15 zaouias (tombs of saints, including Sidi Magdoul, the one who gave the city its previous names), two catholic churches and four synagogues.

Ben Youssef Mosque Laid out in traditional fashion and located on the Medina's main boulevard is one of the most important, and impressive, in the city (not open to non-Muslims).

Kasbah Mosque Just off the main square, the mosque dates back to the days of the city's reconstruction (not open to non-Muslims).

La Synaogogue de Simon Attias As Essaouira was a trading city, many of its inhabitants were Jews, living primarily in the Mellah, at the north end of the Medina. Most left by the 1960s migrating to other countries, especially Israel or the United States. This 19th-century remainder in the heart of the Medina is one of the few synagogues that still stand.

L'Eglise Portuguese South-east of the Medina is this richly decorated Catholic church established by the first European businessmen who settled here in the 18th century.

Skalas

These coastal fortifications are probably the most distinctive feature of Essaouira. Part of the 18th-century redesign of the city, the barrier walls were constructed as defenses, acting as protection against invasions from the sea, and additionally enforced with cannons pointing out towards their attackers. At various points, are 'borj's', fortifications that further enforce security.

Skala de la Kasbah The southwestern-facing barrier provides not only a sense of safety to the inhabitants within its shadow, but also a delightful wall-top walk overlooking the sea. Along the edges are the installed weaponry, while underneath, in the arches, are the studios and shops of woodworkers and cabinetmakers. Orson Welles made much of his 1950s film version of *Othello* here.

Skala de la Port Towering over the fishing port, this huge and intriguing fortification offers great views of both the activities below and the ocean beyond. For a small fee, it's possible to see the construction from the inside. ⏱ Daily 08.00–12.00, 14.00–18.00.

○ *Fortifications – skalas – protected Essaouira from invasion in the 18th-century*

Souks

Much more easy-going, and a lot less claustrophobic than Marrakech, walking through Essaouira's souks is a pleasure. Meandering and maze-like, the shopping experience provides a sense of exploration and discovery. Although based mostly along the main street, shops and markets still sprawl all over the town. Some of the specialist items are: Fabric market (Souk Joutya); Fish

market (marché aux poisons); Grain market (Souk Zraa); Jewellery market (Souk Siagha); and the Spice Market (Souk Laghza).

CULTURE

Art galleries

The city is famous for its artists and there are several formal art galleries, as well as impromptu displays laid out on the streets. Some of the venues double as shops, while others are purely exhibition areas. The Taros Café presents world music and musical evenings, alongside its visual arts and commercial interests (ⓐ place Moulay Hassan 2, rue Skala ① 044 47 64 07). The Exposition de l'Ensemble Artisanal is another place to see traditional, handmade crafts and get a guide to the quality and price of items out in the souks (ⓐ avenue Mohammed El Kourri, Bab Marrakech ① 044 47 22 71).

Gnaoua Festival

This festival, held annually in June, celebrates Gnaoua, a traditional music genre that has captured the imagination of many of the West's more mainstream musicians. For four days, exponents of the pure form show off their technique while foreign performers join in to create fusion. Started in 1998, this event has been gaining momentum and becoming more popular, and more crowded, every year. ⓦ www.festival-gnaoua.co.ma

Sidi Mohammed Ben Abdallah Museum
(Musee des Arts et Traditions Populaires)

Named after the sultan who commissioned the 18th-century redesign of the city, this museum is the only formal one in town. It specialises in Moroccan ethnography and includes displays on

musical instruments, 19th- and 20th-century fashion, mostly silver jewellery and furniture constructed from the local thuya wood.
ⓐ 7 Derb Laalouj ⓣ 044 47 23 00 ⓛ since 2005, the museum has been undergoing restoration.

RETAIL THERAPY

Arga'Dor Various products made with the oil from the fruit of the native Argan tree are for sale here, including soaps, scents and even honey. ⓐ 5 rue Ibn Rachid, Medina ⓣ 061 60 14 71.

Bazar Tilili Pottery items are stacked up and crammed into every available space, in both the traditional Fes, and the more modern Safi styles. ⓐ souk de poisson (epices), 55-Souk-el-Jadid, Medina ⓣ 068 94 50 66.

Ben Chibat Abrahim Inside this narrow passage is a small store selling brightly coloured *babouches* (slippers) made from raffia: something a bit different from the usual. ⓣ rue El Hajali, Medina (across from the Perle Restaurant, at no. 2) ⓣ 066 78 38 79.

Chez Samir All sorts of Moroccan bits and pieces are sold, ranging from carpets to artisan objects. Most interesting are the coloured powders from which artists' paints are made, including the ground-up shell Murex blue. ⓐ 16 rue Ibn Rachid, Medina ⓣ 068 51 77 67.

Grand Choix Among the usual articles carved in the local Thuya wood are miniature guitars, clearly a tribute to the city's most famous visitor of the 60s, Jimi Hendrix. ⓐ 5 rue Laalouj, Medina ⓣ 044 47 54 85.

L'Art du Bain Artisan soap makers create bars in all shapes and sizes and in a huge range of fabulous scents – go in for a sniff. ⓐ 41 La Scala ⓣ 068 44 59 42 (also in Marrakech: ⓐ 32 Marché Central de Guéliz, rue Ibn Toummert ⓣ 068 44 59 42) ⓦ www.lartdubain.com

Meditel It looks like a mobile phone shop, but this little place also covers most photographic needs, dealing with both analogue and digital photography. ⓐ rue Attarine, Medina ⓣ 044 47 20 29.

Super Marché Attisir This large supermarket, where most of the usual edibles are available, is located in the new town ⓐ 287 blvd Al Aqaba, Lottisement 5 ⓣ 044 47 29 94.

Tamouzika Tailors and sewing machine operators produce reasonably priced, high-quality leather bags, jackets, trousers and waistcoats, sold both off-the-peg and bespoke (ready the next day). ⓐ 5 rue Laalouj, Medina ⓣ 044 47 38 84.

Youssef This little kiosk hidden inside the ramparts is full of CDs from both the West and the Maghreb (Algeria, Libya, Morocco and Tunisia). Youssef is friendly and knowledgeable, especially regarding Gnaoua music and the annual festival. ⓐ 1 place Chefchaouni, Medina ⓣ 062 83 50 32.

TAKING A BREAK

Chez Driss Essaouira's most famous pastry shop has been in business since 1928, and its beautiful cakes are still created under the influence of its French origins. Relatively pricey but delightfully atmospheric. ⓐ 10 rue El Hajali ⓣ 044 47 57 93 ⓛ 09.00–18.00.

● *Blue and white seem to typify the town, but shops add a touch more colour*

Chez Kanane At this charming café/restaurant, situated on a little square just within the ramparts, you can have your orange juice, mint tea, or even something more substantial, outside on the place or within the traditionally decorated interior. ❷ 2 place Chefchaouni ❶ 063 38 74 32.

Fish market stalls Between place Moulay Hassan and the port are these stalls where each vendor displays his catch and offers to cook whatever you choose in any quantity in any fashion. Sit at the tables provided and enjoy the freshest fish and seafood imaginable, while watching others do the same. ● 12.00–22.00.

Taros Café As well as an artistic and musical venue, the café serves alcohol at its bar, together with the more usual beverages – sit below, on the square, or above, on the terrace. ⓐ place Moulay Hassan 2, rue Skala ❶ 044 47 64 07.

Tassaout One of the many places to linger and enjoy the life of the main square, it's easy to spend a long time here, sipping and nibbling as the day goes by. ⓐ 10 place Moulay Hassan ❶ 071 52 23 13.

AFTER DARK

Chalet de la Plage D (DD with wine) Another local institution, the beachside restaurant first built in 1893 still serves excellent seafood and has great views. It's less crowded in the evening, when the day-trippers have gone. ⓐ avenue Mohammed V ❶ 044 47 59 72 ⓦ www.lechaletdelaplage.com

Chez Sam D (DD with wine) Way down at the end of the fishing port is an Essaouira legend, serving seafood and decent wines in a boat-shaped venue. ❸ at the bottom of the Port du Peche ❶ 044 47 62 38.

Le Patio D (DD with wine) Within a riad, the tapas restaurant menu changes daily, comprising whatever fish have been taken from the sea that day, as well as the more usual tagines. ⓐ 28 rue Moulay Rachid, Medina ⓣ 044 47 41 66 ⓛ Tues–Sun 17.00–23.00.

Les Alizes Mogador D Cheap and cheerful, this small place hiding within the seawall of the Skala de la Kasbah serves Moroccan dishes ⓐ 26 Rue Skala ⓣ 044 47 68 19.

Le Homard Maajoune DD This restaurant, hotel and gallery, serves fine gourmet cuisine in a beautiful 18th-century building that was once the Italian consulate, just next to the main square. ⓐ 2 rue Mehdi ben Toumert ⓣ 044 47 52 62.

ACCOMMODATION

Hotel Shahrazed D Basic and inexpensive, the location is excellent, right next to the main tourist office. ⓐ 1 rue Youseef el Fassi, Medina ⓣ 044 47 64 36.

Palazzo Desdemona D (DD suite) Sprawled around a large central courtyard with each spacious room equipped with a four-poster bed, this traditionally decorated hotel faces on to the Medina's main thoroughfare. ⓐ 12–14 rue Youssef El Fassi, Medina ⓣ 044 47 22 27.

Riad al Madina D In a *riad* dating from the late 19th century, though having gone through various facelifts since then, the hotel is still famous for some of its 1960s clientele, including Jimi Hendrix, Jefferson Airplane and Frank Zappa. ⓐ 9 rue Attarine, Medina ⓣ 044 47 59 07 ⓦ www.riadalmadina.com

Villa Maroc DD Four 18th-century houses have been joined together

to form a delightful Hispano-Moorish style boutique hotel. One of Essaouira's most legendary small hotels. **ⓐ** 10 rue ben Yassine **ⓣ** 044 47 61 47 **ⓦ** www.villamaroc.com

Sofitel DDD This large four-star hotel located alongside the sea has full luxury facilities including a spa and swimming pool, private section of beach, and windsurfing equipment rental. **ⓐ** avenue Mohammed V **ⓣ** 044 47 90 00 **ⓦ** www.accorhotels.com

Campsites

There are several campsites in the general area, although some are a little way out of town:

Camping le Calme 150 spots include 100 for motor homes and 50 for tents. **ⓐ** 15 km (10 miles) south-east from the centre, on the route to the village of Arba Ida ou Gourd **ⓣ** 044 47 61 96.

Camping les Oliviers The campsite comprises 100 places. **ⓐ** 21 km (13 miles) east, on the road to Ounagha **ⓣ** 062 35 37 47.

Camping Sidi Magdoul Of the 100 pitches, 60 are for motor homes, and 40 for tents. **ⓐ** 1 km (0.6 miles) south, on the route d'Agadir, next to the Marabout Sidi Magdoul **ⓣ** 044 47 21 96.

Camping Tangaro Smaller than some of the other sites, there are 80 spaces with 60 for motor homes and 20 for tents. **ⓐ** 6 km (4 miles) south on the road to Agadir-Diabat **ⓣ** 044 78 47 84.

▶ *Surf the net out of doors at Marrakech's Cyber Parc (see page 151)*

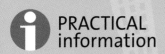

Directory

GETTING THERE

There are various ways to get to Marrakech, depending on how much time you have and how much you would like to see en route.

By air

It's possible to fly nonstop to Marrakech's **Menara Airport** from London Gatwick as well as a few major European cities, including Paris. Most flights, however, stop over at Casablanca. Airlines that cover this route include Atlas Blue (w www.atlas-blue.com), GB Airways (as part of British Airways, w www.gbairways.com) and Royal Air Maroc (w www.royalairmaroc.com). From the USA, Royal Air Maroc has a nonstop routing from JFK Airport in New York to Casablanca, with connections available at either end.

By rail

All trains that traverse Morocco are domestic. The easiest way to get to Marrakech from Europe is to take the ferry crossing from Spain over the Gibraltar straits to Tangier, and head to Casablanca, from where there is a direct line to the Guéliz railway station. Although tracks exist, there have been no border crossings from Algeria since 1994. The Moroccan rail network is efficient and has an excellent website at ⓦ www.oncf.ma

By boat

There are several companies that do the crossing including Euroferrys. From Algeciras, the regular boat cruise takes about 4 hours, although there is also a faster catamaran. ☏ 34 9 7 658841 ⓦ www.euroferrys.com. Ferries Rapido del Sur does a quick crossing to Tangier: from Tarifa it takes 35 minutes, from Algeciras 70 minutes and from Gibraltar 80 minutes. For Spain ☎ 34 956 68 18 30 and for Morocco 212 39 94 26 12 🌐 www.frs.es/eng/index.htm.

Sailing to the quieter port of Ceuta might be a better option especially when travelling by car, as there is less traffic, but not so good for foot traffic, as there are fewer public transport connections than from Tangier. If time is not a problem, and a 36-hour sea journey is preferable to a drive, boats also leave from Sete in France and sail to Tangier: Comanav ☎ 39 010 582080 🌐 www.comanav.co.ma

By car

If you're looking for the fastest way, once across the straits, get to Tangier (via the N16 from Ceuta) then take the coastal motorway, the N1, to Casablanca. From there, drop south on the N11, which becomes the N9 and a regular road at Settat, all the way to Marrakech. For more details, contact the Touring Club du Maroc ☎ 044 27 92 88.

Package deals

There are over a hundred UK-based operators that offer tours to Morocco, of which more than a dozen provide short-break options to Marrakech. Among the many is Thomas Cook Holidays ☎ 01733 418 200 🌐 www.thomascook.com.

TRAVEL INSURANCE

Travel insurance is essential, especially in Morocco, where medical facilities do not match those of developed countries. There are no reciprocal arrangements for EU members. In the case of a serious incident, it's probably best to fly home, or to the nearest western

European country, for proper treatment. It's also advisable to be financially covered in the case of travel delays and in the unlikely event of major theft.

ENTRY FORMALITIES

There are no visa requirements for stays of up to three months for citizens of the following regions: Australia, Canada, the European Union (except foreign nationals living in the Republic of Ireland), New Zealand, the UK and the USA. South Africans, and non-citizens residing in the Republic of Ireland, need to contact their embassies or consulates for further information. All visitors require a passport that is valid for at least six months after their date of entry into Morocco.

Customs

Personal effects, including cameras (for non-commercial use) are allowed into the country duty free. Adults are allowed to bring in one bottle of wine and one bottle of spirits. The tobacco allowance is 200 cigarettes, or 50 cigars or 250 grams of tobacco.

MONEY

The dirham is the official currency in Morocco. One dirham = 100 centimes, although finding things to buy for denominations of less than 1 dirham is rare. Coins come in 5, 10, 20 and 50 centimes, and 1, 5 and 10 dirham. Notes come in units of 20, 50, 100 and 200 dirham.

Moroccan money is not allowed out of the country and should be purchased on arrival and resold (if any is left) before departure. Make sure all exchange is done officially at banks, bureaux de change and hotel cashiers, rather than illegally on the street, especially with traveller's cheques. Receipts issued on the initial transaction are required when changing money back. EU currency is commonly accepted, especially when buying items at the souks, and prices are often quoted in euros.

Most towns have banks that almost always include exchange bureaux. ATMs are reasonably common, especially in the cities. On weekends, both locals and tourists line up at the available cash dispensers, so try to make sure your money supply is topped up during regular banking hours.

Credit cards are accepted at many of the finer hotels, restaurants and shops. Even some souk stalls will take them, and their use can become part of the bartering process – if you are too keen on the item and the seller knows you are dependent on the credit, his price may not be very negotiable. At the same time, if you're unsure about the item and he's not flexible, it's very easy to walk away and find someone else who is happier taking the card.

HEALTH, SAFETY & CRIME

Even though it's ostensibly a developing country, Morocco is reasonably safe. There are no vaccinations suggested for people either going to, or coming from, the country, and anti-malaria prophylactics are not needed.

However, even though tap water is treated, it's still best to drink bottled water. Make sure the seal is unbroken before taking a swig. Also, do not drink water from rivers, even fast-flowing mountain streams. Fruit and vegetables should be washed and, where possible, peeled.

Sun protection is important, especially during the summer. Make sure you use suntan oil or block and that you have enough to last for the entire stay. Don't spend too long outdoors, particularly at midday. At all times of the year, swim only in hotel pools, secure beaches and safe areas of coastline.

Morocco adheres to the Islamic beliefs of hospitality and respect, without following some of the more militant fundamentalist trends. Western visitors are encouraged and welcomed. Wandering around Marrakech tends to be very safe, even for women. However, there are always some basic rules that ought to be followed. Dress should be dignified while in the city and especially the Medina, avoiding wearing clothes that are appropriate only for the swimming pool or the beach. At the same time, don't overdress, or wear too much jewellery, and don't carry more money than is necessary for a day out.

It's easy to get lost, particularly at night, but try to avoid areas that are poorly lit. If confused, ask for directions before entering a dark and deserted area. Police are around, although not usually visible. To discourage the hassling that used to go on several years ago, tourist police now operate – successfully – undercover and only appear when needed. Most of the locals know this fact, and behave accordingly.

OPENING HOURS

Banks are open every day but Sunday, with hours varying as follows: Mon–Thur 08.15–12.15, 14.15–17.15; Fri 08.15–11.15, 14.00–17.30 Sat 09.00–13.00.

Post offices are open from Mon–Fri 08.00–12.00 and 14.00–18.30, Sat 08.00–14.00. The main one is in Guéliz, at place 16 du Novembre, along avenue Mohammed V, and the Medina branch is on rue Moulay Ismail, between the Jemaa el Fna and the Koutoubia. If you ever want your postcards to arrive, it's best to send them from here, rather than from the forlorn boxes scattered through the city.

Typical opening times for both government and private offices are Mon–Thur 08.00–12.00, 14.00–18.30, Fri 08.00–11.00, 15.00–18.30.

Shops set their own hours, but usually the larger stores are open 09.00–13.00, 15.00–19.00 every day but Sunday, while the souks take every opportunity to make money and function daily 08.00–13.00, 14.00–18.00.

Museum times also vary locally, but in general their hours are Wed–Mon, opening between 08.30 and 09.30 and closing between 17.30 and 18.30. More as a rule than an exception, they close for an hour at lunch. For more specific information, contact the Ministry of Culture ⓘ 037 20 94 00.

TOILETS

Public toilets are not common, and it's usually best to stop in at a decent café, or even a hotel, to take care of this need. The attendant will expect a tip. Try to carry a packet of tissues, as away from the better places it's up to you to provide the supply. Plumbing is poor, and the basket you see next to the toilet is for used paper. The facilities at the airport are fine.

CHILDREN

Marrakech is not particularly oriented towards children, and there are very few activities specifically designed for them. They are generally allowed at restaurants, although no special concessions are usually made for young ones. The exception to this indifference is at kid-friendly McDonald's, and there are two of these in Marrakech: one around the huge place du 16 Novembre in Guéliz and the other close to the Marjane supermarket on the Casablanca road.

The city's two hypermarkets, Marjane on the Route de

Casablanca and du Metro on the route de Fez, have the largest selection of things for children. Unitex, in Gueliz, specialises in clothing for children ❷ 35-36 ave Moulay-el-Hassan, Centre Kawkab ❶ 044 43 04 65. The shop Articles pour le Bebe has things for babies and is in the new city, on 68 rue de la Liberté ❶ 044 43 12 00, in Guéliz. The souks are full of goods and colours that fascinate visitors of all ages, and it's possible to find a toy or item that will delight little ones, although the closeness of the markets can be a little scary.

What appeals to the inner child also works for the outer one, and the Jemaa el Fna is full of attractions for everyone. Children like the monkeys and snakes that appear in the square during the day, as well as the dancers and singers. Slightly older youngsters appreciate the night activities, enjoying the acrobats and performers just like the older folks do.

Caléche rides are fun for kids as well as for parents, and the carriages can take a whole family at one time. Some of the horses pulling the carts are very well kept and nice to pet. Playgrounds are relatively rare, but the Jardin Harti in Guéliz has two facing slides disguised as dinosaurs having a head-to-head. On Friday and Sunday, both children and adults like feeding the gigantic carp with even bigger appetites in the reservoir at the Royal Palace's Agdal Gardens.

COMMUNICATIONS
Phones
Payphones work with phone cards that are sold at kiosks and tourist shops around town. Teleboutiques are also very common. Marked

❶ *Signs point the way to necessities of life*

GOOD LOOK
Pret à Porter
Feminin

TELEPHONE

FAX

INTERNET

صانع الأسنان

DENTISTE

طبيب

DOCTEUR

ECOLE DIDI
ETABLISSEMENT
PRIVEE
de Coiffure

outside by a blue sign, these privately run shops have individual secluded booths and a person is on hand to offer change and advice. Prices are very reasonable and it's often easier to find these boutiques than a public phone. Mobile phones function if they are compatible with Morocco's two GSM networks. The national networks have excellent coverage throughout the country.

To make a call outside Morocco, first dial the outgoing international code of 00, then the country code. For Australia, it's 61, for Canada and the USA, 1, for the Irish Republic 353, for New Zealand 64, for South Africa 27 and for the UK 44. The number for international phone enquiries is 120 and national ones 160.

For calling Morocco from abroad, dial the local international code then 212. Drop the first zero listed for domestic calls, then the local code then the number. For example, the number for the Marrakech Tourist Office when dialled within the country is 044 43 61 31, but to phone from the UK would be 00 212 44 43 61 31.

Post

Marrakech's main post office is in Guéliz, and there is a large sub-branch just off the Jemaa el Fna in the Medina. Local kiosks and tourist shops also sell stamps. One for a postcard sent anywhere out of the country costs 6.50, and it can take up to week for the card to arrive in Europe, further away, somewhat longer. Post boxes are yellow and say 'Poste' on them but there is a chance that a postcard dropped in one of these mail slots, rather than sent from a post office, may never arrive.

Internet

Using the internet is becoming very popular, with access available all over Morocco. Many hotels offer connections as part of their services, sometimes wireless. Outside, access points are advertised on the streets, often alongside the teleboutiques. A few cyber points are:

Café Atlas ❷ rue Bab Agnaou, Kissaria Essalam.

Cyber Parc Arsat Moulay Abdeslam on blvd Mohammed V, just across from the Hotel de Ville (City Hall), this beautifully landscaped park is equipped with Internet access screens that work with phone cards. Not good for surfing at night, but a pleasure to do so by day.

Hotel Ali ❷ rue Moulay Ismail, Medina 📞 044 44 49 79.

ELECTRICITY

Electricity here works on the same system as the rest of Western Europe, with 220 volts (AC) and 50 hertz in new buildings, although some older buildings and smaller villages still work on 110V. The standard two-pin round-ended adapters used for the Continent are required for UK and USA electrical items.

TRAVELLERS WITH DISABILITIES

Marrakech is not particularly easy for disabled tourists, as there are virtually no special adaptations in place for them. The Medina's streets are rough, often unpaved and crowded, with oblivious foot traffic. The newer, larger hotels have special access, particularly those belonging to the larger chains.

Some of the traditional *riads* have ground-floor rooms with most of the activity based round the central courtyard, so minimal mobility is not such a problem. Riding in a horse-drawn carriage is a good way around the city, and these *calèches* will venture even into some of the smaller streets of the Medina. More information can be found at ⓦ www.holidaycare.org.uk

🔻 *Bureaux du tabac are the places for a postcard or newspaper*

TOURIST INFORMATION

Marrakech The city's main tourist office is located in the heart of Guéliz ⓐ place Abdelmoumen Ben Ali ☎ 044 43 62 39.

Essaouira The Regional Tourist Office and Tourist Information Centre is just inside the City Walls ⓑ 10 rue de Caire, BP 261 ☎ 044 78 35 32.

Websites

There are many excellent websites describing Marrakech, its sights, *riads* and restaurants. Some of them are:

www.ilove-marrakech.com
www.morocco.com/destinations/marrakech
www.riadsmorocco.com
www.al-bab.com/maroc/trav/marrakesh.htm;
www.tiscali.co.uk/travel/eworldguides/travel/marrakech_travel.html

FURTHER READING

Many classic works are from writers who have passed through and been inspired by Morocco and its charms. A few are:

Hideous Kinky Esther's Freud's 1992 semi-autobiographical work about being an English child in 1970s Marrakech was turned into a movie by Giles MacKinnon six years later.

Naked Lunch William Burrough's drug classic of 1959 was written while the writer was living in Morocco.

The Sheltering Sky Paul Bowles's beautiful and chilling novel, written in 1949, was made into an equally impressionable film by Bernardo Bertolucci in 1990.

The Voices of Marrakech Elias Canetti wrote this poignant series of stories about his visit 14 years before winning the Nobel prize for Literature.

Useful phrases

Although Arabic is the official language of Morocco, and English is spoken in some tourist areas, French is spoken widely. These words and phrases may come in handy.

English	French	*Approx. pronunciation*
BASICS		
Yes	Oui	*Wee*
No	Non	*Nawng*
Please	S'il vous plaît	*Seel voo pleh*
Thank you	Merci	*Mehrsee*
Hello	Bonjour	*Bawngzhoor*
Goodbye	Au revoir	*Aw revwahr*
Excuse me	Excusez-moi	*Ekskeweh mwah*
Sorry	Désolé(e)	*Dehzoleh*
That's okay	Ça va	*Sahr vahr*
To	À	*Ah*
From	De	*Der*
I don't speak French	Je ne parle pas français	*Zher ner pahrl pah frahngsay*
Do you speak English	Vous parlez anglais?	*Voopahrlay ahnglay?*
Good morning	Bonjour	*Bawng-zhoor*
Good afternoon	Bonjour	*Bawng-zhoor*
Good evening	Bonsoir	*Bawng-swah*
Goodnight	Bonne nuit	*Bun nwee*
My name is ...	Je m'appelle...	*Zher mahpehl ...*

English	French	*Approx. pronunciation*
DAYS & TIMES		
Monday	Lundi	*Langdee*
Tuesday	Mardi	*Mahrdee*
Wednesday	Mercredi	*Mehrkrerdee*
Thursday	Jeudi	*Zhurdee*
Friday	Vendredi	*Vahndrerdee*
Saturday	Samedi	*Sahmdee*
Sunday	Dimanche	*Deemahngsh*
Morning	Le matin	*Ler mahtang*
Afternoon	L'après-midi	*Lahpreh meedee*
Evening	Le soir	*Ler swahr*
Night	La nuit	*Lah nwee*
Yesterday	Hier	*Yehr*

English	French	Approx. pronunciation
Today	Aujourd'hui	*Ojoordewee*
Tomorrow	Demain	*Dermang*
What time is it?	Quelle heure est-il?	*Kel urr ehteel?*
It is ...	Il est...	*Eel eh ...*
09.00	Neuf heures	*Nurv urr*
Midday	Midi	*Meedee*
Midnight	Minuit	*Meenurhee*

NUMBERS

One	Un/Une	*Ang/Ewn*
Two	Deux	*Dur*
Three	Trois	*Trwah*
Four	Quatre	*Kahtr*
Five	Cinq	*Sangk*
Six	Six	*Seess*
Seven	Sept	*Seht*
Eight	Huit	*Weet*
Nine	Neuf	*Nurf*
Ten	Dix	*Deess*
Eleven	Onze	*Awngz*
Twelve	Douze	*Dooz*
Twenty	Vingt	*Vang*
Fifty	Cinquante	*Sangkahnt*
One hundred	Cent	*Sahng*

MONEY

I would like to change these traveller's cheques/this currency	J'aimerais changer ces chèques de voyage/ ces devises	*Zhaymray shahngzheh seh shek der vwahahzh/ seh derveez*
Where is the nearest ATM?	Où se trouve le distributeur de billets le plus proche?	*Oo ser troov ler distribewter der beeyeh ler plew prosh?*
Do you accept credit cards?	Vous acceptez les cartes de crédit?	*Voos aksepteh leh kart der krehdee?*

SIGNS & NOTICES

Airport	Aéroport	*Ahehrohpohr*
Rail station/Platform	Gare/Quai	*Gahr/Kay*
Smoking/non-smoking	Fumeurs/non fumeurs	*Fewmurh/nawng fewmurh*
Toilets	Toilettes	*Twahlayt*
Ladies/Gentlemen	Femmes/Hommes	*Fam/Ommh*
Subway	Métro	*Maytroa*

Emergencies

EMERGENCY NUMBERS
Fire brigade (pompiers) ☎ 15
Ambulance (SOS accident circulation) ☎ 044 40 14 01
Doctor (24 hr) ☎ 044 40 40 40
Medical emergencies (Urgences médicales) ☎ 044 44 79 99
Police ☎ 19
Highway emergency services ☎ 177

HEALTH
All doctors and dentists speak French, a few speak English. Ask at the tourist office, your hotel or *riad*, or at the consulate. In emergencies, consular services will usually be able to help.

Pharmacy (24 hr) ➋ rue Khalid ben el Oualid ☎ 044 43 04 15

Hospitals
Clinic al Koutoubia ➋ rue de Paris, Hivernage ☎ 044 43 85 85
Polyclinic du Sud ➋ rue du Yougoslavie, Guéliz ☎ 044 44 79 99

Dentist (English-speaking) Dr Youssef Dassouli ➋ Residence Asmae, apt 6, 1st floor ☎ (emergency) 064 90 65 14.

LOST PROPERTY
Lost and found (Objets trouvés) ☎ 044 44 79 10

CONSULATES & EMBASSIES
There is a British Honorary Consul in Marrakech ➋ Residence Jaib 55 Boulevard Zerktouni ☎ 044 43 60 78 (emergencies only).

The following have their representation in Rabat, Morocco's capital:

Canada 🏢 13 bis Rue Jaafar Assadik, Rabat 📞 037 67 28 80
🌐 www.dfait-maeci.gc.ca

South Africa 🏢 34 Rue des Saadiens, Rabat 📞 037 70 6760
🌐 www.dfa.gov.za

UK 🏢 17 Ave. de la Tour Hassan, Rabat 📞 037 73 14 03
🌐 www.britishembassy.gov.uk

USA 🏢 2 Ave. de Marrakesh, Rabat 📞 037 76 22 65
🌐 www.usembassy.ma

Australia Refer to Australian Embassy 🏢 4 Rue Jean Rey, 75724 Cedex 15, Paris, France 📞 33 1 4059 3300 🌐 www.france.embassy.gov.au/
New Zealand Refer to New Zealand Embassy 🏢 3rd floor, Plaza de La Lealtad 2, 28014 Madrid, Spain 📞 34 915 230 226
🌐 www.nzembassy.com

EMERGENCY PHRASES

Help! Au secours! *Ossercoor!*

Fire! Au feu! *Oh fur!*

Stop! Stop! *Stop!*

Call an ambulance/a doctor/the police/the fire service!
Appelez une ambulance/un médecin/la police/les pompiers!
Ahperleh ewn ahngbewlahngss/ang medesang/lah poleess/leh pompeeyeh!

The publishers would like to thank the following individuals and organisations for supplying their copyright photographs for this book. Ethel Davies: all images except:
A1 Pix: pages 5 and 8.

Copy editor: Deborah Parker
Proofreader: Jan McCann

Send your thoughts to
books@thomascook.com

- **Found a great bar, club, shop or must-see sight that we don't feature?**

- **Like to tip us off about any information that needs a little updating?**

- **Want to tell us what you love about this handy little guidebook and more importantly how we can make it even handier?**

Then here's your chance to tell all! Send us ideas, discoveries and recommendations today and then look out for your valuable input in the next edition of this title. As an extra 'thank you' from Thomas Cook Publishing, you'll be automatically entered into our exciting monthly prize draw.

Email the above address (stating the title) or write to:
CitySpots Project Editor, Thomas Cook Publishing, PO Box 227, Unit 15/16, Coningsby Road, Peterborough PE3 8SB, UK.